# HANDBOOK OF
# BASKETBALL DRILLS

from

## *The Coaching Clinic*

# HANDBOOK OF
# BASKETBALL DRILLS

Compiled and Edited
by the Board of Editors

Parker Publishing Co., Inc.

**from The Coaching Clinic**

**of The Coaching Clinic**

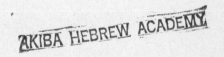

**West Nyack, New York**

HANDBOOK OF
BASKETBALL DRILLS
fr m
*The Coaching Clinic*

Compiled and Edited by
the Board of Editors
of
*The Coaching Clinic*

© 1972 BY

PARKER PUBLISHING COMPANY, INC.
WEST NYACK, NEW YORK

LIBRARY OF CONGRESS
CATALOG CARD NUMBER: 70-161894

PRINTED IN THE UNITED STATES OF AMERICA
ISBN 0-13-374124-9
B C

# Introduction

Here are some of the best basketball drills selected from over 500 articles that have appeared in the monthly publication, *The Coaching Clinic*.

Forty-three of basketball's top high school and college mentors combine to demonstrate (with over 250 illustrations) their drills and techniques for perfecting all aspects of the game.

You'll find drills for warm-ups and conditioning, tailor-made offensive and defensive drills, and multiple-purpose drills to fit any style of play.

Whether you're new to coaching basketball or an established veteran, the *Handbook of Basketball Drills from The Coaching Clinic* will help you and your players master the fine points of the game—and keep you on the winning side of the ledger.

Board of Editors
*THE COACHING CLINIC*

# CONTENTS

## OFFENSIVE DRILLS: THE FAST BREAK

# PART III

## DEFENSIVE DRILLS

## PART IV

## COMBINATION DRILLS

# HANDBOOK OF
# BASKETBALL DRILLS

from

## *The Coaching Clinic*

# Part I

## WARM-UP AND CONDITIONING DRILLS

# 1

## WARM-UP DRILLS

### by Kevin Trower

*Head Basketball Coach*
*De LaSalle (New Orleans, Louisiana) High School*

Kevin Trower has been coaching high school and college basketball since 1959. He was assistant basketball coach at Loyola University, head coach at Jesuit (New Orleans, Louisiana) High School, and assistant coach at Louisiana State University. At present, he is head basketball coach at De LaSalle High School. The following article is based on his coaching at Jesuit High School.

J esuit High emphasizes defense. We are even "emphatic" enough to include a couple of defensive drills as part of our pregame warm-up routine. Since defensive work as part of a pregame warm-up is rare—at least in our area—our drills draw ridicule from opponents and their fans. And that is but one reason why we do them. It has become a point of fierce pride to our boys and to our fans, and it makes us feel a few jumps ahead of our opponents.

We always do the drills after lay-up shooting. Do not do them when your boys are still cold, as they are quite vigorous.

### DEFENSIVE DRILL 1

Form two lines out-of-bounds under the basket on either side of the lane, as shown in Figure 1. Starting position is even with the backboard, facing the base line, inside foot on the three-second line. Keep knees bent, butt low, and feet comfortably spread. Arms should

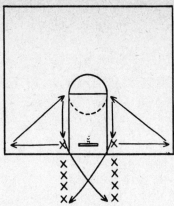

**Figure 1**

be loose in front of you. To begin, step out toward the sideline with the outside foot.

### Coaching Point

Your first move is a step. Do not bounce with both feet on the first move. On the first step, your inside foot will still be on the floor, so that, if the imaginary offensive opponent had faked you to the sideline, you would still be in a position to move back to the inside with him after his fake. If you bounced to the sideline on his fake, you would be vulnerable to the inside. After your first step, if you (watching his belt buckle) see that he is really going to the sideline, then you can move out with him. Stepping, instead of bouncing, makes you less vulnerable to a fake. This is a point well-learned in the drill.

Use a boxer's glide-step (do not cross legs). Keep knees bent, the butt low, and move as fast as possible. Watch where you are going out of the corner of your eye, and put your outside foot right on the sideline.

When your outside foot hits the sideline, swing your inside foot back, and slide back in the opposite direction, angling your path toward the intersection of the foul line and the three-second line.

After swinging your foot back and changing direction, glide-step as fast as possible to the edge of the foul line. Watch out of the corner of your eye so you can put your inside foot right on the intersection of the foul line and the three-second line. When your inside foot hits the intersection, push off of your inside foot and spring out fast down the three-second line toward the base line.

The next boy in the drill will be in the starting position, with his back to you, waiting to go. See how fast you can react after you hit the foul line. Sprint out toward the base line and slap the next boy on the butt with your outside hand. This is his signal to step out toward the sideline and begin his turn in the drill. You move to the end of the opposite line.

### DEFENSIVE DRILL 2

Use the same starting positions as in drill 1. To begin, run backwards to the half-court line. Get up on your toes and move. Lean forward slightly from the waist, to keep from losing balance and falling on your butt.

When you get to the half-court line, bounce into a defensive stance and touch both hands to the floor. Feet should be spread, butt low, and knees bent.

After touching the floor with both hands, bounce into position and employ the boxer's glide-step out to the sideline as fast as you can move your feet. Put your outside foot right on the sideline. Immediately push off that foot, changing direction quickly, and glide back in toward the center circle.

Watch out of the corner of your eyes and put your

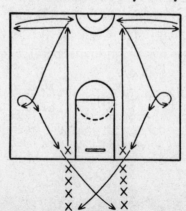

Figure 2

inside foot on the edge of the center circle. Immediately push off that foot, and sprint for the intersection of the sideline and the base line (the corner) closest to where you originally started from.

When you reach approximately the foul-line extended area, get low and make a full back pivot on your inside foot —swinging your outside foot all the way around until your feet are pointed toward the basket. Your body will resemble an automobile swinging all the way around in reverse gear. Head for the next man who is in position, waiting to go, with his back to you. He is facing the base line, ready to run backwards to the half-court line. Get to him as fast as you can. Slap him on the butt with your inside hand, which is his signal to begin. You move to the end of the opposite line.

# 2

# PREGAME DRILLS

## by Earl Reddish

*Head Basketball Coach*
*Cambridge (Maryland) High School*

Earl Reddish started his basketball coaching career at North Dorchester (Hurlock, Maryland) High School. In his last year there, his squad won the district play-offs. He later moved to Bowie (Maryland) High School and then to his present post at Cambridge High School.

It's my feeling that many basketball games are won during the 20 minutes of pregame drills. At least, it has worked that way for us over the last few seasons.

This phase of the game is definitely overlooked by the beginning coach. It's up to him to see that his players take such drills seriously, and that they execute them in a quick, snappy manner.

Here are some pregame drills that helped my squads in the beginning—and they are still helping us now. In each drill, look for running, ball handling, and shooting. You rarely win games any other way.

### TWO-BALL LAY-UP DRILL (DIAGRAM 1)

Run this one for seven minutes: #1 passes to #2; #4 passes to #3; #2 passes to #4; #3 passes to #1; #2 and #3 follow and get the rebound; #1 and #4, after the lay-up, take the two post positions; #2 goes to the end of #4's line; #3 goes to the end of #1's line.

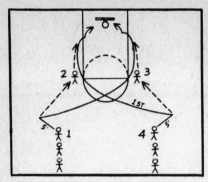

Diagram 1

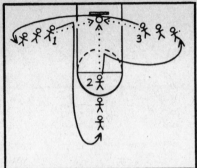

Diagram 2

## THREE-BALL JUMP-SHOT DRILL

Run as shown in Diagram 2 for four minutes, then as shown in Diagram 3 for four minutes: #1 takes the shot, retrieves the ball, and bounce-passes it back to his line. After this, he rotates to his right. At the same time, #2 and #3 are executing the same action.

After completing the above three drills, the players should be sufficiently "warmed up" to go on to more strenuous drills. Every coach should realize the importance of the warm-up period, which is designed to prevent injuries.

### RUNNING DRILL (DIAGRAM 4)

Run for one minute: The first time run backwards; second time run sideways; third time run forward hard. #1 and #2 must start this drill at the same time.

Diagram 3

Diagram 4

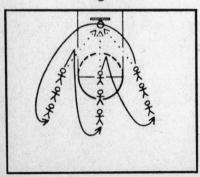

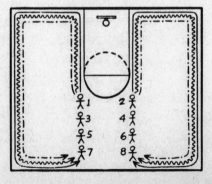

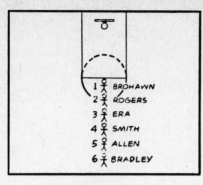

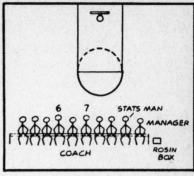

| Diagram 5 | Diagram 6 |

## FOUL SHOOTING (DIAGRAM 5)

In the remaining four minutes, the team works on foul shooting and favorite "spot" shooting. Have your first six men shoot as many fouls as time will allow. Set up the squad by numbers so that each player automatically knows when it's his turn to shoot. This helps keep the drill moving.

## BENCH PROCEDURE (DIAGRAM 6)

Every new coach should stress the importance of bench procedure to his squad. It's necessary to maintain discipline and keep the players alert as to what's going on out on the court, because a player never knows when he might be called upon to go into the game and do a job.

Keep the number 6 and 7 men next to you. If it's necessary to substitute, they are close by for instructions. This also enables you to keep your eyes on the court and talk to them at the same time. Make sure that the manager has rosin, towels, and gum for the players. The statistician should be recording rebounds, assists, etc.

Have your "starters" lie down on the floor in front of the bench during the time-outs (Diagram 7). This extra rest will come in handy during that crucial fourth quarter—and

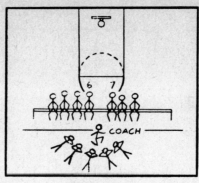

**Diagram 7**

be sure you have a clipboard ready to draw a play or cover future strategy during such times.

These drills and procedures will not guarantee any coach a winning team—but if performed properly, they will certainly contribute to building a winning team and program.

# 3

# PRESEASON CONDITIONING DRILLS

by F. Dwain Lewis
and Douglas Sanderson

*Head Basketball Coach and
Assistant Basketball Coach
University of California at Riverside*

F. Dwain Lewis is assistant athletic director at the University of California at Riverside, and Douglas Sanderson is the assistant basketball coach at the same institution. Their cooperation in many research efforts on proper conditioning has resulted in fruitful results, and their thinking has been adopted by others in basketball. Their overall record is 115–62.

**B**asketball cannot be played in low gear; that means a team must be in prime condition for the opening game or pay a penalty. Attaining condition in the early part of the competitive season means games will be surely lost.

Preseason training obviously is the remedy, and we have developed a physical fitness program that is rough but gives a player a feeling of accomplishment. It is a stiff enough drill routine to cause less-motivated players to cut themselves from the team and leave the workers.

## THREE POINTS

We believe our program helps us in three ways: (1) in building strength and endurance by isometric, isotonic, and running drills; (2) in injury prevention; (3) in team discipline. We have not had a muscle sprain, shin splint, or a case of blisters in a two-year span with this program.

The drills are done in the order cited below to allow for maximum organization efficiency and to provide rest intervals.

## TWO-WEEK PERIOD

In the first week of the two-week drill period, the players perform exercises at three-quarters speed for 30 seconds and at full speed for the final 30 seconds of the one-minute drill.

In the second week there is no letup, and all drills are performed with maximum effort for the whole minute.

## TIME SPAN

The program takes about 35–40 minutes daily, approximately the length of time a player would work in a game.

It is organized in such a way that the first 20-minute period aims at strength development, while the final 15–20 minutes stresses endurance.

### Stretching

Standing position, right leg over left leg, left hand over right shoulder. Bend over and pull down, touching toes for 30 seconds. Reverse feet and hands for 30 seconds.

### Chair

The player assumes a sitting position against a wall, with knees at right angles and hands not on the knees. The player's back in its entirety should be touching the wall.

Leg pressure is applied pushing back against the wall, ranging from about three-quarter effort the first few sessions to maximum in the second week.

### Splits

The player assumes a standing position with legs as wide apart as possible, feet parallel and stationary. Pressure is applied by the legs trying to bring the heels together.

Ground resistance puts most of the pressure on the medial thighs. Widen the legs for the last 30 seconds.

### Finger Push-Ups

From the splits position, the player assumes a push-up position on fingertips. The minimum is ten the first day, with one added each succeeding day.

### Ankle Rotation

The player lies on his back and places both hands under his buttocks. The legs are raised about 6 inches and both ankles are rotated in the same direction, with as little leg movement as possible.

This drill also serves as an excellent conditioner for the stomach muscles.

### Pulls

One player lies on his stomach with his legs bent at the knees, at right angles. Another player kneels behind him and pulls against his heels, while the man on the floor resists.

This is a two-minute rather than the usual one-minute drill, because the men exchange places immediately to repeat the exercise.

### Pushes

This is the reverse action of the pull drill. The prone player is in the same position, but the second man pushes against the upraised feet rather than pulling. The men exchange positions.

In both pulls and pushes, the floor man should not be allowed to rest his head in his hands. His knees should be in contact with the floor or ground.

### Rag Tag

One player assumes a defensive stance, with one hand on the shirt of the offensive player. The other hand stays behind feeling for a screen.

The offensive man slides right, left, forward, backward, trying to lose the defensive man, who attempts to maintain contact.

### Shadow Boxing

Two men spar open-handed for quickness with no solid hits. They are instructed to try not to blink or duck away.

Emphasis also is placed on proper footwork for balance and in refraining from crossing the feet while sliding.

### Leap Frog

Two players alternate jumping over each other, with legs spread as wide apart as possible when going over. One partner must go over twice to change direction and keep the drill in a small area.

### Turns

Players perform 180-degree jumps as quickly as possible, getting maximum height every time. Direction must be switched to avoid dizziness. Turns are increased to 360 degrees the second week.

### Up and Back

The player performs a standing broad jump forward and backward, with feet kept parallel.

Each jump should be a gathered maximum effort to encourage balance and good jumping motion.

### One-and-Three-Quarter-Mile Run

This exercise is based on the premise that athletes who can run a mile-and-three-quarters under 12 minutes are in excellent shape for basketball.

The times are recorded each day and adjusted daily according to what the coaches think the player should achieve, which is usually five seconds lower than the previous effort.

The running is done on the grass surface inside the track, and after the first day we like everyone to run barefoot to toughen the feet.

# Part II

## OFFENSIVE DRILLS: GENERAL

# 1

# TAILOR-MADE OFFENSIVE DRILLS

## by Gus Ganakas

*Head Basketball Coach*
*Michigan (East Lansing, Michigan) State University*

Gus Ganakas coached at East Lansing (Michigan) High School for eight years (compiling a record of 180–50 which included eight consecutive conference championships and one state title) before coming to Michigan State University in 1966 as assistant basketball coach. This past season Coach Ganakas assumed the head coaching position at that university.

"It isn't what you do, but how well you do it." "It is not the basketball offense you use, but how well you play it." I believe in both of these "adages." The success of any offense depends entirely on how precisely each player or combination of players execute their moves. Precise execution is achieved through practice—*the way it will be in the game.*

## REVERSE ACTION

Since we have used Pete Newell's reverse action and other complementary offensive moves with success, we find that there are *basically* only two motions in our offense— forward-center-forward (FCF) and guard-guard (GG). For this reason, we have chosen drills that best develop these group motions. They are also drills that make optimum use of court space, because we can have one group practice their motion on one end of the court and the second group practice on the other.

Here is how we work our drills.

### FORWARD-CENTER-FORWARD DRILL

Diagram 1 shows the basic motion for the FCF drill, and Diagram 2 illustrates the continuity of motion upon reversing the ball.

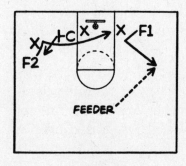

**Diagram 1**

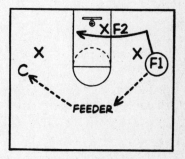

**Diagram 2**

In Diagram 1, a feeder passes to F1 (a forward) who receives the pass after first executing the proper fundamentals of creating the lead and pass reception. C (the center) sets a screen facing the ball, positioning himself along the foul lane. F2 (the second forward) deploys his defensive man to the lateral line of the screen. Using a change of direction, F2 cuts across the screen either over or under. He is the first cutter and C (the center) becomes the second cutter.

Upon reversing the ball the motion is continuous, with the center occupying F2's position and F2, who broke across, assuming the screening position (Diagram 2).

Second cutter routes, illustrated in Diagrams 3, 4, and 5, are threefold:

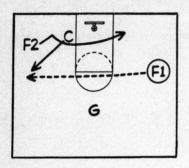

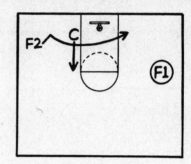

Diagram 3                                        Diagram 4

### Diagram 3

The second cutter (and screener) opens up the court by breaking to F2's original position. If the passing lane to the center is open, the forward (F1) will pass cross-court.

### Diagram 4

He can break to the weakside post position looking for the short cross-court pass from F1. Also, after reversing the ball to the out guard, an effective weakside two-on-two operation can be exploited by the center and guard.

### Diagrams 5a and 5b

The third option the cutter has is to break to the ball either high or low, depending on the first cutter's route. This has been an especially effective move against a switch.

The FCF drill has a multi-purpose function since many basketball fundamentals are practiced. It disciplines timing of the pattern; encourages individual development by creating one-on-one situations; teaches change of direction, cutting, and offensive and defensive rebounding.

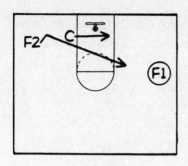

Diagram 5a

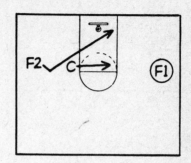

Diagram 5b

## GUARD "DOVETAIL" DRILL

While the front line is working on the FCF drill, the guards use the other end of the court for a two-on-two drill which incorporates a guard maneuver in our offense.

Diagrams 6, 7, and 8 show this guard play called guard "dovetail." There are three options to look for:

**Diagram 6**

G1 passes to G2 and cuts away. This cut-away keys the move. The first option is to hit the cut-away man (GI).

Diagram 6

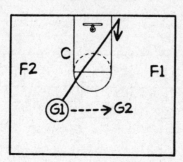

### Diagram 7

G2 attempts to drive into the vacated guard area cre-
ated by G1's cut-away.

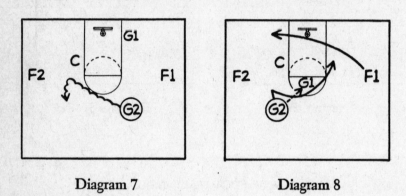

Diagram 7                              Diagram 8

### Diagram 8

The third option, and the completion of this two-man
guard maneuver, is for G2 to pass to G1 who has since dove-
tailed to the foul-line post position. G2 executes a change of
direction, for timing as well as deception purposes, and then
cuts off the post into the open side which was vacated by F1
(played by one of our second team).

The two-on-two "dovetail" drill trains the guards to
drive, dribble with the outside hand, feed post, and change
direction. Also, since the guard group is together, time can be
given for a two-on-two or three-on-two drill operating against
a press.

The guards work on bringing the ball up the court
from the base line to midcourt against either two or three
defensive men, who play both man-to-man and zone. This is
an invaluable drill for training guards to operate against the
press with proper individual and two-man techniques.

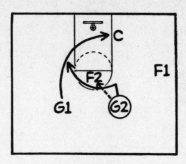

Diagram 9

Of course, our offense is not based entirely on forward-center-forward and guard-guard moves. We have many guard-forward and guard-center moves that are incorporated into the offense.

The guard-forward pass fundamentals, including the pass, pass reception, and associated footwork, are stressed continuously in our one-on-one and guard-forward two-on-two drills. The entire reverse-action pattern is initiated by a guard-forward move called guard around. The guard and forward exploit this two-man move before any cutter action takes place. It is most important that the first cutter does not make his cut until the guard and forward have had an opportunity to express themselves by the guard-around maneuver.

The guard-center pass is considered one of the guard's passing lanes. It is looked for when the forward's lead is cut well. From here, the guard's scissors cut off the post is used. The forward on the weak side often breaks to the foul-line post position. From this alignment, the guards also cut in the routes shown in Diagram 9.

# 2

# SINGLE-PIVOT OFFENSE DRILLS

**by Phil Anderson**

*Former Head Basketball Coach*
*Paxton (Florida) High School*

Phil Anderson's 17-year coaching record at Paxton High School is 299–158. He has also collected a good share of district, conference, and state championships in that time. Phil Anderson resigned from high school coaching in 1968 to enter politics. At present he is Clerk of Circuit Court for Walton County, Florida.

Our basic offense here at Paxton High School is the "single pivot." It's made up of simple offensive maneuvers involving guard-forward-pivot men. We use eight drills to help us perfect this offense. Here, they are numbered one through eight for the purpose of practice only.

We begin these drills in the seventh grade, so they become automatic through the years. Therefore, we are able to run them on the move and without setting and calling out a number.

Here is how we work our drills.

**Diagram 1**

This is a guard-around play in which the defensive man is brushed on the forward. The right forward moves upward toward the guard to receive the ball. The offense should keep spread out as much as possible to allow more room for the play. The right guard fakes

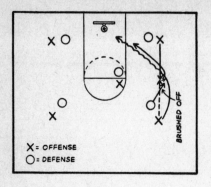

**Diagram 1**

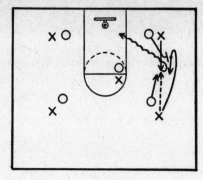

**Diagram 2**

a pass to the center and passes the ball to his forward. After passing, the guard fakes inside and runs to the forward's outside to receive the ball. In doing this, the guard brushes as close as possible to the forward to get loose from his defensive man. After receiving the ball from his forward, the guard drives straight for the basket for a lay-up. After handing the ball off to the guard, the forward trails him to the basket in case he is needed to rebound or in case the guard should want to flip a pass over his head to the trailing forward.

### Diagram 2

This shows a guard-around with the forward's defensive man switching to take care of #1 play. The forward keeps, pivots, and drives hard to the basket. The guard continues toward the corner and back out. The forward comes toward the guard and receives the ball. The guard, after passing the ball, breaks by the forward but does not get the ball. After the guard gets past the forward, he pivots and comes back to where the forward is stationed with the ball. The forward fakes a handoff to the guard but keeps the ball and pivots toward the basket where he drives for the lay-up. This play can be done on either side of the court.

### Diagram 3

This is a guard-to-forward maneuver. The forward takes one dribble toward the center; guard around, but defensive men cannot afford to switch. The forward hooks to the guard on the way in. The right forward moves upward toward the guard, where he receives the ball.

After the guard passes the ball he runs by the forward, brushing close to him in an effort to lose his defensive player. The forward dribbles once to his right and passes a hook pass to the guard who goes for the lay-up.

The hook pass is very effective, as there will be a defensive man on the forward and the hook is almost impossible to block. This play can be done on either side of the court.

### Diagram 4

The defensive man on the guard goes straight down to protect the base. The guard cuts hard toward and by the forward about one step and pivots to the outside, where the forward hands off. The guard shoots a set over the forward or he could drive for a lay-up. The right forward comes toward the guard and receives the ball. After it has been received by

| Diagram 3 | Diagram 4 |
|---|---|

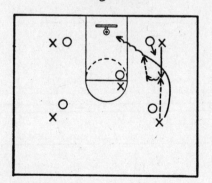
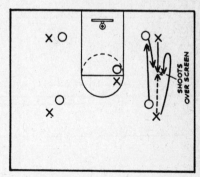

the forward, the guard runs past him but turns and comes back to receive the ball. The guard can either drive for a lay-up or shoot a set shot. This play can be completed on either side of the court.

### Diagram 5

The ball goes directly to the pivot man. The guard screens for the forward; the forward cuts around the pivot for a handoff. The guard cuts, making a simple criss-cross.

Options are numerous. If the ball goes to the forward and he passes to the pivot man, the guard sets up inside the screen and reverse-rolls out for the pass from the pivot. The forward cuts off the screen around the pivot.

There is the simple criss-cross of the forward and guard at the post. The center serves as a screener. The guard passes the ball to the center. The forward and guard then criss-cross on the post where the center can either hand off to one of the two or shoot a turn-around jumper. This play can be executed on either side of the court.

### Diagram 6

The ball goes to the forward; the guard cuts around; the defensive men switch. The guard dribbles about one time,

| Diagram 5 | Diagram 6 |
|:---:|:---:|
| 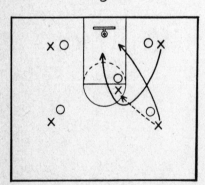 | 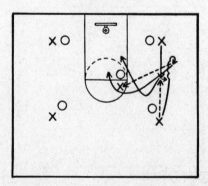 |

pivots away from the defensive men, stays low, and uses a bounce pass to get the ball to the pivot man. In the meantime, the forward has gone two or three steps toward midcourt, reverses, and cuts hard off the guard, who is cutting around the pivot man. The forward comes out and meets the ball passed by the guard. The guard, after the pass is made, cuts by the forward. The guard receives the ball from the forward and dribbles once or twice, pivots to the outside, and passes the ball to the post man. Meanwhile, the forward has ventured out a few feet toward midcourt. The forward and guard now cut and criss-cross on the post. The center can either hand off to the cutting players or shoot a turn-around jump shot. This can be done on either side of the court.

### Diagram 7

This play is utilized when the post man is up high. A simple criss-cross is made by the guards; the forwards come out. It can be continued with the forwards now cutting; the guards come back out. The guards move in fairly close to one another. The right guard dribbles toward the left guard, who in turn moves to the outside of the right guard. The right guard fakes a pass to the left guard and delivers a bounce pass

Diagram 7                    Diagram 8

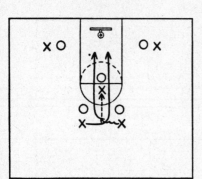

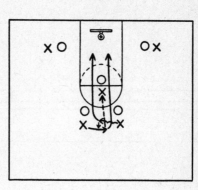

to the center. The two guards then criss-cross on the post. The center can either hand off to one of the guards for the lay-up or pass the ball back out. This play can also be started from the left side

### Diagram 8

This shows a guard dribbling to the left and handing off to another guard hitting the post man, both guards then cutting for the basket. The right guard dribbles toward the left guard, who comes to the right guard's outside. The right guard hands off to the left guard, who in turn throws a quick pass to the center. The two guards then break on the post. The center can either hand off for the lay-up or bring the ball back outside.

# 3

# DRILLS FOR THE SHUFFLE OFFENSE

## by Tracy Walsh

*Assistant Basketball Coach*
*Flathead (Kalispell, Montana) High School*

Tracy Walsh graduated from Anaconda Central Catholic (Montana) High School and—after college and a four-year coaching assignment at Great Falls (Montana) Central—returned to his alma mater as head basketball coach. Despite coaching a small school in a big 32-team classification group, he saw his share of winning seasons. At present Coach Walsh is at Flathead High School. The following article is based on his coaching at Anaconda.

Two years ago, we lost an important conference game just because our offense "slowed down" in the last quarter. Realizing that our problem was lack of movement and sound offensive fundamentals, we searched for a new offensive pattern with good movement and possibilities for better shots.

The shuffle offense was the answer. Finding this pattern effective with the freshmen, we tried it in a few varsity games and finally employed it completely this past year. It has worked wonders for us.

Running this offense takes patience, discipline, and constant drill. Here are some of the drills we use and recommend to perfect the fundamentals.

### PASSING DRILL

Our first practices are devoted to fundamental drills in passing (Diagram 1) — stressing good form and a variety of snappy passes: chest pass, bounce pass, overhead two-handed pass, and the basketball pass, using both the right and left hand.

### SPLIT-VISION DRILL

We use a split-vision drill (Diagram 2), first with heavy basketballs then with regulation ones. Our passes must be snappy and chest high. Every man on the squad gets his chance to be the "middle man."

These drills are run for short periods of time and changed daily to eliminate boredom.

### SHOOTING DRILL

Shooting drills begin early in the season and continue throughout the year. We concentrate on correctly gripping the ball and proper stance, form, and follow-through—while stressing that the boys shoot close to the basket (Diagram 3), gradually moving out.

**Diagram 1**

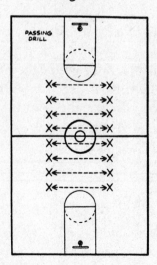

**Diagram 2**

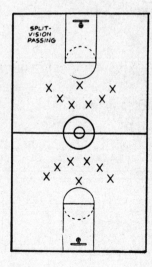

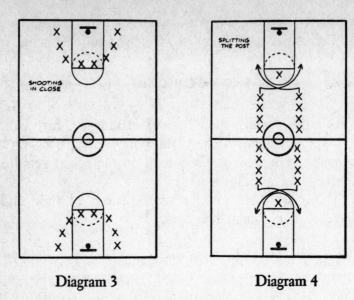

Diagram 3                    Diagram 4

### SPLIT-THE-POST DRILL

Our split-the-post drill gives us practice in moving, passing, receiving a pass, correct takeoff, and shooting. Even our poorest shooters gain more confidence in taking the shot and, as a result, have become fine shooters. We run this split-the-post drill from the top of the key and both sides of the free-throw lane (Diagram 4). One or two basketballs may be used.

After completing our fundamental drills, we begin our offensive drills—emphasizing the following: memorization of the spots, snappy and outside passes, bringing the man into the screen (applicable for the man without the ball), the "square off" before taking the shot, and knowledge of and confidence in our offense.

### HITTING OUR "A" MAN

Our first offensive drill stresses hitting our man on both sides of the free-throw line with the pass on the outside.

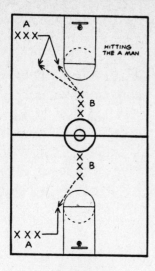

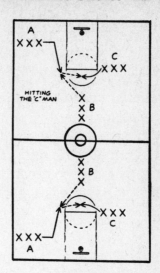

Diagram 5                    Diagram 6

We concentrate on passing to "A," receiving the pass, the pivot by "A," and the shot (Diagram 5). "A" line shoots; "B" line tips and rebounds.

"A," moving until he frees himself from his defensive man, breaks to the free-throw line extended, receives the pass on the outside, pivots, and squares himself with the basket.

Although we want "A" to take a good jump shot at first, he may do the following: (a) reverse-pivot when he receives the ball if he feels his defensive player is checking him too high; (b) "square off" with the basket and drive for a lay-up; (c) take a jump shot if his defensive player has ⁀sagged; (d) pass to any of the cutters.

### HITTING OUR "C" MAN

Our next drill is hitting the "high post" or "C" man, moving across the top of the screen (Diagram 6). We continue to pass into our "A" man and he, in turn, passes to our post, moving across the top of the key. We take this shot from the free-throw line. Later in the screen, we allow our high-post man to drive on a one-and-one situation or other options we have introduced. Timing is an important key in this drill.

We continue the different drills in our breakdown offense until we feel we are ready to incorporate all phases of the offense into our drill program. Demanding that the boys follow the normal offense with a few free-lance drills, we constantly work on movement, timing, and shooting. Thirty to 45 minutes a day are devoted to practicing our offense. During this entire procedure, the pattern "change-over" is being developed.

# 4

# FUNDAMENTALS AND DRILLS FOR THE JUMP SHOT

by Nolan Mecham

*Head Basketball Coach*
*Snakeriver (Moreland, Idaho) High School*

Nolan Mecham's six-year record as head basketball coach at Snakeriver High School is 102–100. The 1969 season was his best to date: a 25–5 mark which included the league, district, and state AA titles. His 1970–71 season record was 19–9, with league and district championships and a fifth-place state finish.

There is only one way to shoot a basketball —the fundamentally correct way. I do not believe in the philosophy that "if it goes in it's okay." I have never seen a consistent 40% shooter who didn't have correct fundamentals.

For the jump shot, perhaps the most important shot in basketball today, learning first things first is a must—if a boy expects to master the shot.

Here are the fundamentals and drills we stress for jump shooting. They are taught at every grade level, starting in junior high.

### TEACHING THE BEGINNER

Our initial instruction is in a passing drill setting (Figure 1). This we find most effective because the boys concentrate on performing fundamentals correctly rather than on making the shot.

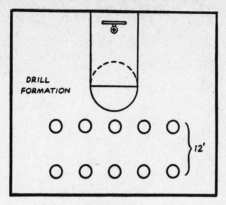

**Figure 1**

1. In our passing drill for the set shot, we stress the following points: (a) left foot forward, right foot back; (b) elbow close to and in front of body; (c) fingertips centered on the ball. (d) "Y" between the thumb and index finger as the ball is brought in front of the right eye. This position puts the fingers on the side of the ball. When the arm is straightened, it will move as it does in a boxing jab so that the fingers are directly behind the ball at the time of release; (e) Cock the hand so you can see wrinkles on the back of the wrist; (f) as the arm is straightened, the wrist will snap forward—the straightening of the arm will naturally bring the fingers directly behind the ball for the release and follow-through; (g) the ball is brought to a position in front of the face centered between the left eye and the right shoulder, and high enough so that the player can just see his partner over the ball.

2. In our passing drill for the jump shot, we stress the same points as for the set shot, excluding (a) and (g), plus the following: (a) The ball position is: ball above head, centered between left eye and right shoulder; (b) feet are parallel 12″ to 18″ apart; (c) ball is released when shooter is completely extended; (d) height that player jumps is increased as his body balance is increased.

## KEY POINTS

We have found that the following points are the most difficult for the jump shooter to master:

1. Wrist action—Many players use only half of their wrist power because they fail to *cock the hand* so that there are wrinkles in the back of the wrist. Elbow position—the "Y" between the thumb and index finger is important. If a boy places his hand directly behind the ball so he looks into his fingers in the starting position, he will force his elbow out.
2. Follow-through—the arm should be straight and the wrist should be down at the completion of the shot. If this is done, the ball will float to the basket with an easy reverse spin.
3. Shooting at peak of jump—To correct a player who shoots on the way up, we have him place the ball above his head before starting the jump.
4. Floor position—A player should go straight up and straight down. This will increase the accuracy of most players. We place chairs in front of shooting positions to encourage this fundamental.

## JUMP SHOT DRILLS

We feel that a player must be able to shoot a jump shot in three basic situations: (1) from a standing position after a pass; (2) after a drive on the dribble; (3) after receiving a pass on the fast break. The following drills are designed for these situations.

1. Game of 25 (Figure 2)—Shooting spots are marked by X's. A 15- to 20-foot jump shot counts 2 points and a short jump shot off the board counts 1. Each boy tries for 25 points. We stress shooting the short jumper off the backboard. Players shoot in pairs. When the second player receives the pass, he must shoot without taking steps or dribbling.

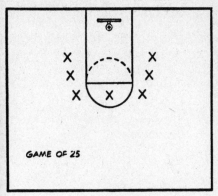

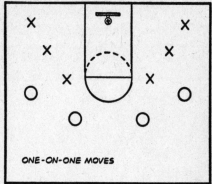

| Figure 2 | Figure 3 |

2. One-on-one moves (Figure 3)—We place chairs or players at the X spots to encourage the boys to go straight up and down. Each boy has a ball and makes a fake at the O spots, then drives to the X spots for the shot. The coach can check the players' concentration on the target area by standing on an X spot and waving his hand across the shooter's eyes. He can also check footwork and fakes at the start of the drive.

3. Fast-break jump shooting (Figure 4)—One ball is used by each pair of shooters. The ball is passed back and forth (usually two passes) and the shot is taken at the top of the key. However, the same drill can provide shots at the X by shifting lines to the side spots on the base line.

**Figure 4**

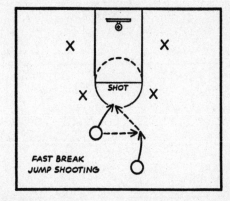

# 5

# REBOUNDING: DRILLS AND TECHNIQUES

**by Larry Randall**

*Head Basketball Coach*
*Jenison (Michigan) High School*

Larry Randall has been coaching high school and college basketball since 1960. He was an assistant coach at Indiana University and Western Michigan University. On the high school level, he coached at Bullock Creek (Midland, Michigan) High School; Jefferson (Goshen, Indiana) High School; Romeo (Michigan) High School. At present, he is athletic director and head basketball coach at Jenison (Michigan) High School. His overall record is 86–34.

As we see it, rebounding is one of the most important aspects of the game of basketball today. The team that controls the rebounds will have control of the ball for a much longer time. In short, we like to run and we are always looking for fast-break opportunities off the defensive board.

We stress that our boys stay relaxed and that they take any open shot when a scoring opportunity arrives. Each boy knows that if the shot is off, someone will be on the board trying for the tip or rebound. We go on the theory that the basket is up there to shoot at —and opportunities to do so must not be wasted.

Our boys are good rebounders because we work on rebounding continually during the season. Here are some of our thoughts, drills, and techniques for this important phase of the game.

## PHILOSOPHY

It's important to organize your rebounding so that the tall boys or the best jumpers are on the boards. Position is very important—so no matter what size you are, keep your boys screened out and stay in rebounding position at all times. Determination and physical strength make for the outstanding rebounder.

The front court boys follow every shot and stay after the ball—as long as there is a chance to get hold of the ball or tie up the defensive rebounder. We always have one guard ready to rebound at the key area and the other guard ready for the fast break on the defensive board. Our guards do not go under and try to board with the horses—for this is a good way to pick up weak fouls and have the other team fast-break you out of the gym.

After every game we post the statistics, so that the players can see the number of offensive and defensive rebounds for the game. We like competition and encourage each player to strive to be the high rebounder for the night, and to go after the rebounding record—a record that has been broken three times this year.

Before covering some of the rebounding drills and techniques that have helped us along the way, remember—a pat on the back is another way to pick up that extra rebound.

## DOG FIGHT DRILL

Our one-on-one dog fight drill (Diagram 1) is good for actual game-type situations, such as basic rebounding, hustling for position, tipping, and defense.

1. Place the boys in two lines facing the basket. The first boy in each line will be standing at the corner of the free-throw line and outside of the lane.

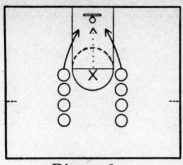

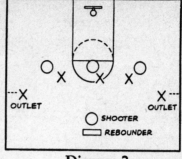

Diagram 1                    Diagram 2

2. A player stands between them and shoots until he makes four baskets in a row—then another player takes his place.

3. Both of the first boys in line break for the rebound, fighting for position. The one who gains possession of the ball tries to tip or lay the ball back up for the basket. If there is no chance for a basket, the boy with possession of the ball becomes the offensive player and the other boy the defensive player—and they play one-on-one until a basket is made.

4. These players then go to the end of the line as the second boys in the line go through the same procedure.

5. The spirit of competition is always good; the team that outhustles the other for ten baskets gets to shoot free-throws while the other team runs 25 to 50 steps.

## FAST-BREAK OUTLET DRILL

The objectives of our fast-break outlet drill (Diagram 2) are to develop rebounding position, to pass to the outlet boys on the side with no dribble, and to have the boys on offense practice their tipping.

1. Divide the boys in teams and place them in position as indicated in Diagram 2—X boys are on defense and O boys are on offense.

2. O shooter is in front of the rebounder machine (Diagram 3) to pull off the ball and shoot a turn-around jump shot.

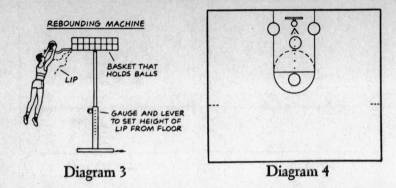

REBOUNDING MACHINE

LIP

BASKET THAT
HOLDS BALLS

GAUGE AND LEVER
TO SET HEIGHT OF
LIP FROM FLOOR

Diagram 3                    Diagram 4

3. When the X boys on defense pick off a rebound, the boy who gets the rebound will pass to one of the outlet fellows to start the fast break. The O shooter (after the shot) will become a defensive player and try to stop the outlet pass to one of the outlet players. Many good fundamentals can be perfected in this drill.

### TIPPING RING DRILL

For this drill (Diagram 4) attach a tipping ring onto the regular goal—and make sure that the ring just allows the ball to fit through it.

1. Place three boys in a triangular position under the goal—one boy will shoot the ball, trying to make a basket at the free-throw line.
2. When the ball comes off the board or rim, the tippers keep it in play until one boy has tipped the ball in.
3. The boys alternate after five balls have been tipped in.

### REBOUND POSITION DRILL

In this drill (Diagram 5), the objective is to give boys practice in moving into the board from a long distance. Make sure that they have good position and are not broad jumping for the ball.

1. The team is divided into two groups and placed in lines that are the forward position in a game; they work high and low from this position.

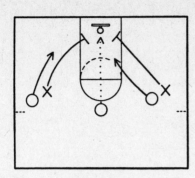

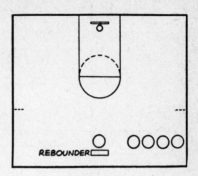

**Diagram 5**               **Diagram 6**

2. The first boy in each line will have his back to the goal and becomes the defensive rebounder. The second boy will be the offensive rebounder.
3. Have a guard practice his shot at the key area. All four boys race for the ball. The defensive players should check out the offensive boy's path.
4. The boys then exchange positions in the lines so that all will get a chance in each position.

### LEGS AND WRISTS STRENGTHENING DRILL

For this drill (Diagram 6), we aim at jumping, ball control, and strengthening the legs and wrists.

1. Place the forwards and centers in one line. The rebounder machine is placed at midcourt; set the lip (which holds the ball) to the height of 9′ 3″ to 9′ 6″ from the floor
2. The first boy in line holds the ball firmly in both hands and faces the rebounder. He then jumps as high as he can and brings the ball off the lip of the rebounder. Each boy does this in sets of 15, 20, 25, and after each set turns and drives hard to the basket for the lay-up. Work for speed and watch that the boy is jumping off the balls of his feet.

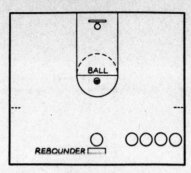

Diagram 7

## SPEED, WRISTS, AND JUMPING DRILL

This is an outstanding drill (Diagram 7) for that second effort in a game. It builds speed, strength for the wrists and legs, and develops a tipping habit.

1. Place the forwards and centers in one line. The rebounder machine is placed at midcourt, and the lip is set from 9 to 10 feet from the floor.
2. Place the ball in the free-throw area. The first boy in the line faces the rebounder and starts jumping as high and as fast as possible, batting the lip of the rebounder with both hands and getting as much wrist action as possible.
3. Each boy does three sets of 15, 20, and 25. After each set, he turns and digs out the ball at the key area, driving hard for the lay-up. The boy rebounds his own shot and places the ball in the key area for the next boy—then he hustles back to the end of the line.

# 6

# DRILLS TO IMPROVE SCORING

## by Michael McHenry

*Head Basketball Coach*
*Rutherford (New Jersey) High School*

Michael E. McHenry played basketball at Carson-Newman College in Tennessee, and became assistant coach in charge of the freshman team at Rutherford (New Jersey) High School in 1967. For his first campaign, 1967–68, Coach McHenry had the honor of guiding a team that recorded a 17–0 record in the Bergen County league and was top seeded in the county tournament. His freshman coaching record is 52–2. At present, he is head basketball coach at Rutherford, with an overall record of 83–14.

The saddest words in basketball are uttered by a coach who claims that his side could have won if it had the ball just once more. He is inferentially admitting that the other side was more efficient with the scoring opportunities that did occur in the game.

We at Rutherford feel that many teams fail to take advantage of plays that may result in a score, and we have devised season-long drills to sharpen our reaction to these opportunities. For example, many teams try to control the tap to get possession, but we try to score off the tap.

### ALERT SITUATIONS

This is one of the situations that an alert team will try to turn into a score. Any jump ball besides the opening tap will serve as an opportunity for us to take advantage of.

Other advantageous situations come on: (1) out-of-bounds plays under the basket;

(2) out-of-bounds plays from the side court; (3) fast break from a missed free throw; (4) fast break from defensive rebound [similar to (3)].

### TAP PLAYS

In Diagram 1, X1 taps the ball to X5. As the ball was tossed up, X2 broke for the basket. X5 passes to X2 for the easy lay-up. The play may be executed to the opposite side.

In Diagram 2, on the toss of the ball X5 breaks for the basket and X1 long-taps to X5 for an easy score. We use this play if we have a mismatch on the jump ball and our advantage is considerable.

In Diagram 3, the play is similar to that in Diagram 2, except that X1 taps the ball to X2 as X5 breaks, and X2 makes the long pass to X5.

These plays may be used at the foul line on a jump ball as well as at center court on the tap.

Diagram 1          Diagram 2          Diagram 3

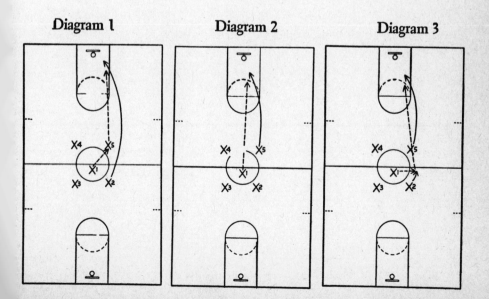

## OUT-OF-BOUNDS, UNDER BASKET

In Diagram 4, on the bounce of the ball by X1 from out-of-bounds, X2 breaks towards the basket, X3 breaks outward, X4 moves towards center at the foul line, and X5 rolls down to the base line.

We want to get the ball to X2 for the easy lay-up, but we also have X5 coming in for a close shot. X3 is the safety valve if X2 and X5 are not open.

### Splitting Defense

In Diagram 5, the middle lane is held by X5 to occupy the middle defensive man. X2 and X4 take positions toward the sidelines to occupy defensive men in those areas and split defense wide.

This opens an opportunity for X3, starting from the foul line, to break to the side of X5 opposite to that taken by his defensive man. If the midcourt defensive man leaves X5 to cover X3, then X5 is open. If he stays on X5, then X3 is open.

### Employing a Pick

In Diagram 6, X4 comes back and picks for X5, and then rolls to the basket. X5 comes off the pick rolling to the basket. X3 goes to the sideline to get out of the way. X2 holds for a deep outlet pass. There is tremendous scoring pressure under the basket for a pass from X1, following the pick by X4.

**Diagram 4**      **Diagram 5**      **Diagram 6**

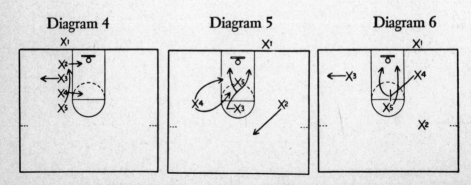

## OUT-OF-BOUNDS, SIDE COURT

In Diagram 7, as X1 passes from out-of-bounds to X4, X2 rubs his man off on X5. Then X4 looks for X2, but he also could pass to X3, who has hooked diagonally back toward center court.

### "Around the Horn"

In Diagram 8, our "around the horn" play off an out-of-bounds pass is depicted. X1 passes in-bounds to X2, who passes to X3. As the ball is passed, X1 runs down the side to pick off in X5's area.

By this time, X4 should have received the pass from X3 and be ready to hit X5 who is cutting. X4 and X1 should crash for the rebound.

## FAST BREAK OFF A FREE THROW

In Diagram 9, our fast break off a missed free throw is shown, which would be the same on a rebound of any shot. When O3 misses the free throw, X1 gets the ball.

X1 tosses to X4 who dribbles and draws O4 to cover him. X4 passes to X3 in the middle lane and he passes to X5 who drives in for the shot.

The key player is X3 who should drive downcourt fast, before O3 recovers.

Diagram 7                Diagram 8 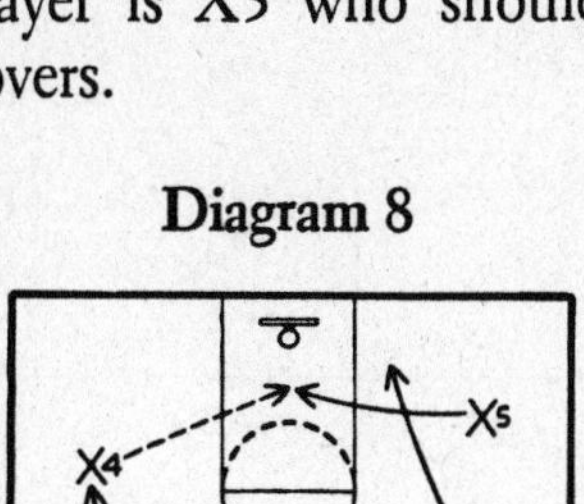                Diagram 9

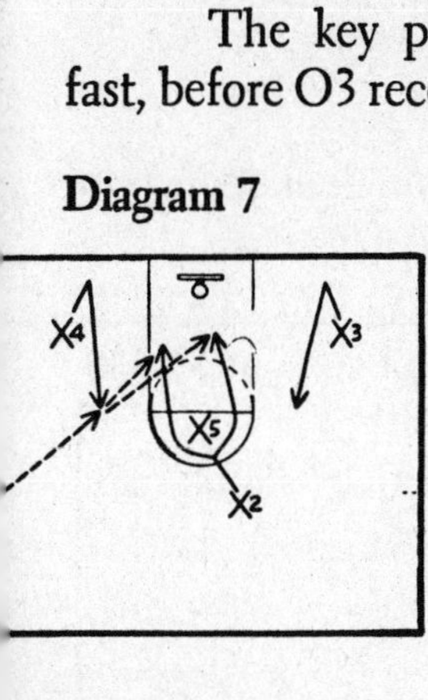

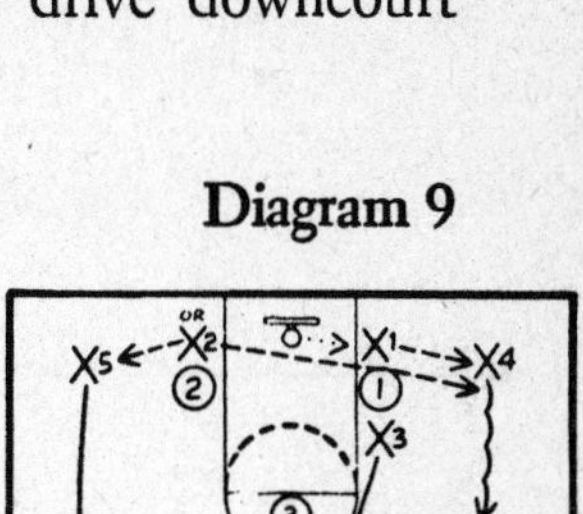

## DRILLS TO GET READY

We practiced the above plays every day and believe they won the close games for us. These were the plays with direct bearing on scoring, but we value the preparatory drills as highly.

Our stress is on leg condition and cardiovascular reading, since basketball is a fast, hard, exhausting game. We inform our boys at the start that they must be prepared to achieve the physical condition that will enable them to outrun any opponent.

Our training session is fast-paced and never lasts more than one hour and 45 minutes, because we believe that is the limit before staleness and inattention set in.

### Three Basic Drills

Underlying our season-long scoring play drills are three basic exercises to develop stamina, quickness, and speed.

In Diagram 10, our touch-line drill is shown. The boys go around the path indicated in squat position, touching the lines with both hands, while using stop-and-slide footwork.

### Four-Point Drill

In Diagram 11, the four-point drill is depicted. The players line up out-of-bounds under a basket. In turn they run to the midcourt line, come back to the foul line, and run behind a manager to the side court, touching the line with both feet. Then the move is completed with a slide-step to the opposite sideline, where three fingertip push-ups are executed. It is important that the player does not cross his feet in this drill.

### Zig-Zags

We call the drill in Diagram 12 the "suicide." It is a zig-zag course down the court, with the player starting at the base line.

He runs out to touch the foul line extended, returns to the base line, runs out to the half-court line, and back to the foul line extended.

Then he runs back to midcourt, and on down to the opposite foul line extended, back to the half-court line, then to the base line, back to the foul line, and returns to the base line. In a final burst, the player runs from this base line back to the base line from which he started.

| Diagram 10 | Diagram 11 | Diagram 12 |
|---|---|---|

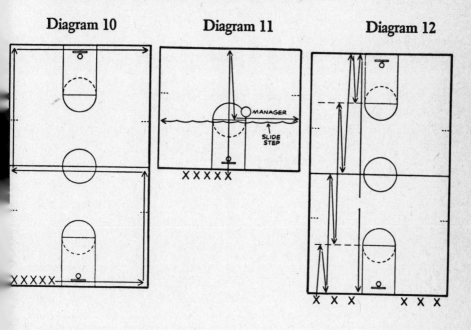

# 7

# THREE-MAN DRILLS

## by Bob Frye

*Head Basketball Coach*
*St. Peters (Mansfield, Ohio) High School*

Bob Frye has coached basketball at St. Peters High
School for the past 13 years. His overall record is
258 wins and 65 losses—this includes ten district
titles out of the last 11 years; four regional titles out
of the last six years; one state championship.

We use three-man basic basketball drills because they make it much easier to teach any new offense, whether it be single post, double post, shuffle, or any other type. That is because the drills, or games, emphasize the fundamentals of cutting, passing, screening, dribbling, rebounding, and shooting that are employed in all systems.

These three-man drills are simple also and may be taught at an early age; we start in the fifth grade of our school system and repeat the drills every year in every grade through high school.

### BASIC ALIGNMENT (DIAGRAM 1)

The normal guard spot is occupied by X1, whose fake is important in starting most drills. If he has the ball, he makes a fake with his head or with the ball; if he has passed off, he must fake one way and go the other, according to the pattern desired.

The forward or wing man, X2, plays halfway between the base line and the foul line extended and about 4 to 6 feet in from the sideline. To receive the ball, he must break to the open area on the foul line extended 4 to 6 feet from the sideline.

The wing must be able to free himself from an over-playing defensive man, usually by a quick jab toward the base line and a hard break to the open area. Another method is to fake coming out and go to the base line for a lob pass.

Center, pivot, or post man X3 must work free once the first pass is made by the guard. He can set his man up with jab steps or fakes so that when he hits the high post he has the defender behind him.

### FIRST DRILL (DIAGRAM 2)

X1 passes to X3 breaking across the key. X1 cuts off X3, setting up with a jab step to run his defensive man into the pivot. X2 waits until X1 cuts, sets up his man with a fake, and cuts off X1 and X3, trying to run his man into the pivot.

### Options

X3 can hand off to X1 and roll to the basket, execute the same play with X2, or drive behind X1 and X2. He also can work for a jump shot in the key area should defense sag a little.

Diagram 1

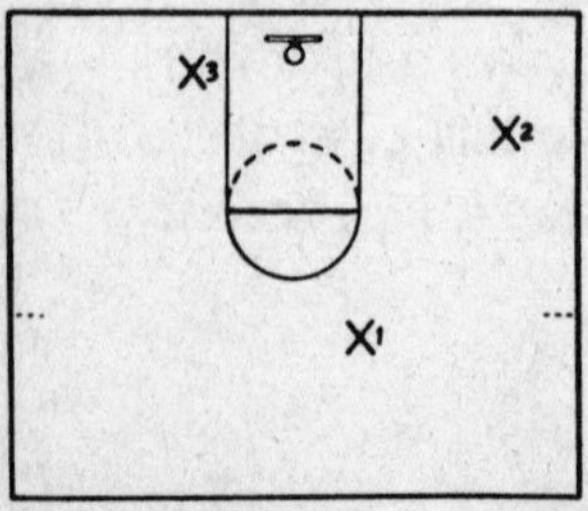

Diagram 2

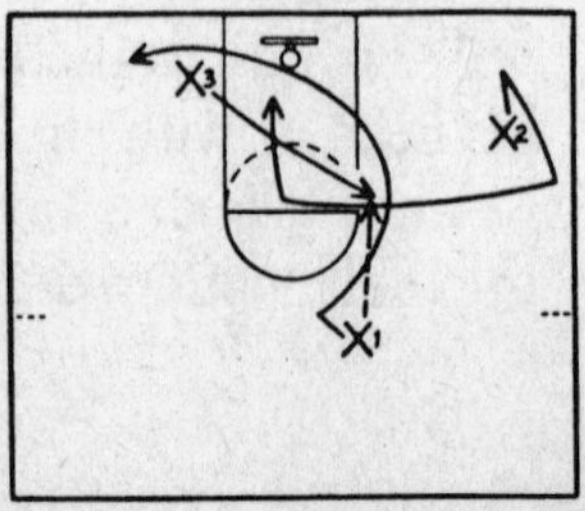

## SECOND DRILL (DIAGRAM 3)

X1 passes to X2 and waits; X2 passes to X3; X2 cuts off X3; X1 waits until X2 cuts and then cuts off X3.

### Options

X3 can hand off to X2 and roll to the basket, execute the same play with X1, or look for a defense sag so as to drive behind X1 and X2 for a shot from the key area.

## THIRD DRILL (DIAGRAM 4)

X1 or X2 passes to X3, breaking to the high post. If X1 passes first, he breaks first, off the high post, going through to the basket after a fake or jab step to set up his man. X2 then breaks in the same pattern. If X2 passes first, he cuts first.

### Options

X3 can hand off to the first cutter or to the second, or turn around and give an overhead return pass to X1 or X2. He also can take the opportunity, if offered, to drive behind the cutters and take a short jump shot from the high post or key area.

Diagram 3           Diagram 4

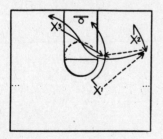
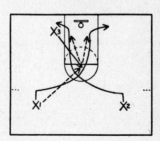

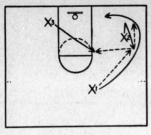
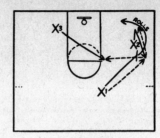

**Diagram 5**            **Diagram 6**

### FOURTH DRILL (DIAGRAM 5)

X1 passes to X2 and circles behind X2; there is no planned play beyond this point, but a variety of options.

#### Options

X2 can hand back to X1 and set a screen for X1 to take an outside shot or drive off the screen. He can keep the ball and look for a drive or shot. X2 also may give X1 a lead pass, going to the basket along the base line, with X2 then rolling to the basket ahead of his defensive man looking for a return pass. X2 may pass to X3 breaking to the high post and then cut off X3; X3 must delay until X1 and X2 make their cuts and passes first. On the last option, X3 may hand back to X2 or drive, or take a jump shot.

### FIFTH DRILL (DIAGRAM 6)

X1 passes to X2, cuts, and sets up a screen for X2, which opens many opportunities.

#### Options

X2 can take an outside shot, drive off the X1 screen, or pass back to X1 if the latter opts to roll toward the basket. X2 can pass to X3 and cut off X3 to the basket looking for a return handoff; if X3 screens for X2 after X1 rolls out, X2 can then drive off the X3 screen.

# 8

# OFFENSE GEARED TO DRILLS

## by Gerald Jones

*Head Basketball Coach*
*Union (Phoenix, Arizona) High School*

Gerald "Wimpy" Jones has coached at Phoenix Union High School for 12 years and has won four AA state titles and five Christmas tournaments. His Coyote teams won 223 and lost only 64. His overall coaching record after 26 years is 445 wins and 177 losses.

At Phoenix Union, we consider basketball to be a game of 1-on-1, 2-on-2, and 3-on-3. We employ an offense geared to drills based on those situations. Seldom do we use four players on any set play. To round it out, we are basically a fast-breaking ball club and our drills incorporate all the means to score by that direct avenue.

## THE DRILLS

### The 1-on-1 Drill

On the 1-on-1, we have the defensive man about 4 yards from the offensive man (Diagram 1). The defensive man tosses the ball to the offensive man and takes three or four quick steps toward him. This gives the offensive man a definite advantage to drive. Care is taken to watch the pivot foot for traveling violations.

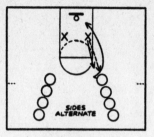

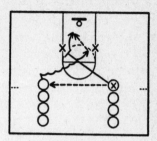

Diagram 1                              Diagram 2

### The 2-on-2 Drill

We work on the pick-and-roll play on our 2-on-2 drills, and practice teamwork to shoot over or drive around (Diagram 2).

### The 3-on-3 Drill

On the 3-on-3 drills, we bring the post man into the play on the split-the-post series. Whoever throws into the post first breaks first, and the third man breaks off his heels (Diagram 3).

### Fast-Break Drills

We have a number of fast-break drills which we work on regularly. The one shown (Diagram 4) is a lane fast break and works this way: The players take lanes, with the ball going to the middle lane by the midcourt line.

Diagram 3                              Diagram 4

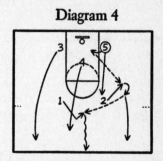

In the diagram, No. 5 rebounds and lets out a pass to No. 2, while No. 1 is breaking for the middle. No. 2 passes to No. 1, or takes the ball to the middle himself. Either No. 1 or No. 2 dribbles to the top of the key on the offensive end— and has the options of passing to either side, shooting, or watching for No. 4 and No. 5 as trailers.

### THE PRACTICE ROUTINE

The importance of the 1-on-1, 2-on-2, 3-on-3, and fast-break situations is illustrated by our typical practice session.

| | |
|---|---|
| 2:15-2:30 | 2-ball lay-in |
| 2:30-2:45 | 3-on-2 fast break |
| 2:45-2:55 | 5-on-2 fast break |
| 2:55-3:10 | 5-on-5 fast break |
| 3:10-3:15 | Break and talk |
| 3:15-3:30 | 1-on-1 |
| 3:30-3:45 | 2-on-2 |
| 3:45-4:00 | 3-on-3 |
| 4:00-4:20 | Against zones |
| 4:20-4:30 | Against presses |
| 4:30-5:00 | 5-on-5 set half-court |
| 5:00-5:15 | Free throws, laps |

Note that most drills are brief, so as not to risk lack of interest and staleness. We also vary the drills and often turn these into contests. This combination holds attention.

### THE OFFENSE

Putting the drills together, our set offense at Phoenix Union is the double post, with the offensive guard who starts the offense going away from the pass. That sets up the 1-on-1 and the 2-on-2 pick-and-roll (Diagrams 5 and 6).

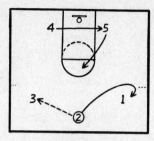

**Diagram 5**

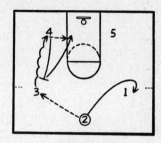

**Diagram 6**

Our formation also sets up the weave offense (Diagram 7) and blends into our stall by moving No. 4 and No. 5 wider to open up the lane. No. 2 passes to No. 3 and breaks opposite, allowing No. 1 to pick the man off No. 2. No. 3 passes into the post, breaks with the pass, and No. 1 goes over the top for a jumper.

### SUMMARY

This is basically the offense we have developed from our essential drills, and we have won two titles in a row with it, against much taller opponents. With two post men we are seldom out-rebounded, and it is easy to switch into a 1-3-1 against zones.

We rely on speed and balanced scoring, and I think our figures are rather remarkable. In our first 11 games in the 1967–68 season, we had six different high-point men.

**Diagram 7**

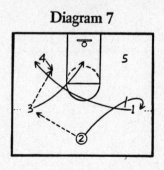

Our team shooting percentage in 1967–68 was 44 per cent on field goals, and 65 per cent on free throws. In 1966–67, our team had a 44.2 per cent average on field goals and 65.7 per cent on free throws. We had only one holdover on the 1967–68 team.

On scoring statistics, the 1966–67 team averaged 75.6 points per game with opponents scoring 60.4 points per game The 1967–68 varsity averaged 72 to 53.3.

# OFFENSIVE DRILLS: THE FAST BREAK

# 1

# ALL-IN-ONE
# FAST-BREAK DRILL

by Art Blecke

*Former Head Basketball Coach*
*Luther North (Chicago, Illinois) High School*

Art Blecke's record as a high school basketball coach is most impressive: a 12-year mark of 212–92 and his share of conference championships. He retired from coaching and is now in an administrative capacity at Antioch (Illinois) High School. The following article is based on his coaching at Luther High School.

At Luther North, we play fast-break basketball—and *mean* it. We believe:

1. The easiest way to score is to get the
   ball down the court before the defense
   *arrives.*
2. If we can't do this, get it there before
   the defense is *set.*
3. If we can't do this, *why waste time?*
   Get that ball down the court anyway.

To do this, we must teach our boys to
react instantly in a planned manner whenever
we get our hands on the ball. We want a controlled explosion toward the basket, triggered
by possession of the ball. Our key is a single
drill. We run it 20 times a day, each practice
session. We feel it gives us that controlled explosion we want *plus:* defensive play, rebounding, ball handling, passing, shooting, and
dribbling—and, it's a good conditioner. Impossible in a single drill? We don't think so.
We also feel that this drill helps us develop the automatic, instantaneous switch

from defense to offense, no matter how we get the ball. The faster the ball starts moving, the better the chance to score. This includes release after a basket or free throw. The *closest* man takes the ball out-of-bounds and gets it back on court *faster than instantly.*

## PRINCIPLE OF THE DRILL

The drill is a perpetual-motion, three-on-two fast break, using the entire squad, offensively and defensively. Three men move down the court with the ball, against two defenders. When a shot is made, or the ball is lost, one of the offensive three drops off the court. A new man joins the two defensive men, and they take over the ball. Thus, they become three offensive men, and move up the court against two new defensive men ready for them at the other end. The two remaining offensive men become defensive men, awaiting the next fast break in *their* direction. When the three new offensive men make a shot or lose the ball, the same procedure is repeated at the other end of the court. Thus, we move up and down the court, without stopping, constantly moving and shifting offensive and defensive men.

## HOW THE DRILL WORKS

We set up as in Figure 1. The three A men are offensive men with the middle man having the ball. The two B men defend. The C men will feed into the drill. The D men are defensive men awaiting the fast break in their direction. The E men will feed into the drill.

I like the ball in the middle of the floor. Therefore, at the start of the drill, the middle A man has the ball, and dribbles downcourt until challenged.

If the defensive men split and do not challenge, the dribbler goes in all the way, and shoots. Normally, he will be

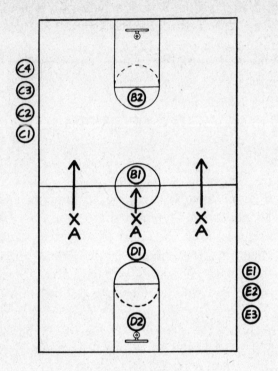

**Figure 1**

challenged at the free-throw line. He will either: (a) stop
and pass to the open man breaking for the basket, or
(b) shoot if the defensive men retreat.

If he is challenged further out than the free-throw line,
he will veer to the most open side, and the wide man on that
side will cut to the middle of the floor *behind* the dribbler
(Figure 2).

As soon as the ball passes midcourt, C-1 moves on the
court and stations himself in back of the free-throw circle. As
soon as an A man scores or loses the ball on a pass or rebound,
C-1 becomes the third man on a fast break upcourt in the
opposite direction (B-1, B-2, and C-1). Men D-1 and D-2
are now in defensive position against this fast break. When

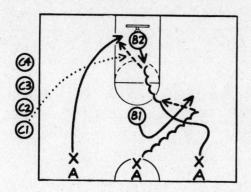

**Figure 2**

the ball passes midcourt, E-1 moves into his position in back of the free-throw circle. He will join D-1 and D-2 as the third man in a fast break in the other direction after a score or loss of ball (by B-1, B-2, and C-1).

In the meantime, the first two boys in the A group who yell "Defense!" stay on the court to defend against the fast break in their direction (D-1, D-2, and E-1). The third A man goes to the end of the C line. Likewise, at the other end of the court after the second fast break, the first two of B-1, B-2, and C-1 who yell "Defense!" stay on the court, and the other goes to the end of the E line.

# 2

# DRILLS FOR INDIVIDUAL FAST-BREAK SKILLS

## by Don Farnum

*Former Head Basketball Coach*
*Benton Harbor (Michigan) High School*

In 18 years of coaching high school basketball, Don Farnum has compiled an overall record of 228 wins against 106 losses. During that time, his squads have captured nine conference titles, six district tourney titles, six regional tourney titles, three runners-up in state finals, and two consecutive state titles. Don Farnum has retired from coaching and is presently teaching at Benton Harbor.

**H**ere are a few special drills we find effective in teaching fast-break skills:

    1. *The Long Pass:* This seems so simple it is usually ignored; yet many coaches have seen baskets lost because the long pass is thrown to a fan in the bleachers. We use this drill to perfect the long pass to the unguarded man (Diagram 1):

Coach throws ball against the backboard. It is retrieved by first man in line A who jackknifes and brings down ball, takes one dribble, and makes a long pass to the first man in line B who broke on the rebound.

    Emphasis is placed on: a baseball throwing motion, no twist of the wrist or arm, and enough arch on the ball to get it over any guard between the two players.

    2. *Multi-Purpose:* We use this drill to improve many phases of the fast break: the

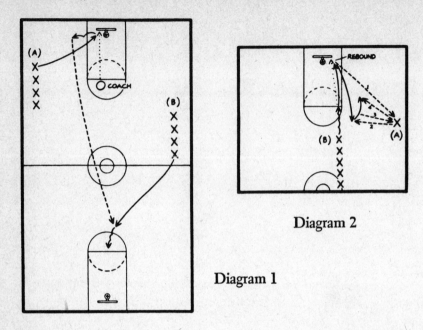

Diagram 2

Diagram 1

outlet pass, ball handling, and quick changes of direction (Diagram 2):

First man in line B dribbles toward the basket, and at the foul line throws the ball against the backboard. He rebounds his own shot, passes out to A, and starts to cut down the floor. A returns ball to B, who stops, passes back to A, and turns back toward the basket. A passes to B, who drives in for the score. After shooting, B replaces A.

3. *Continuous 3-on-2:* After a rebound, we hope to get the opposition in a 3-on-2 situation. This drill conditions our players through constant running, and teaches them to fall into the 3-on-2 pattern automatically when it presents itself (Diagram 3).

No. 1 and No. 2 come out on defense. Nos. 6, 7, and 8 bring the ball down but do not try to score. No. 3 comes off the side and joins No. 1 and 2 in a break the other way. While

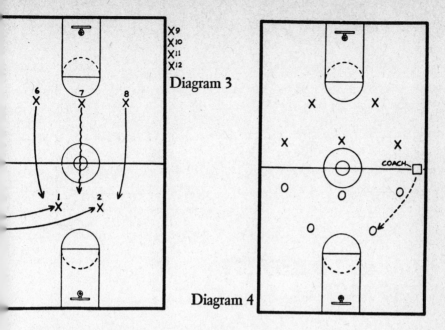

Diagram 3

Diagram 4

the first break has been going on, Nos. 9 and 10 come out on defense. After Nos. 1, 2, and 3 have finished their break, Nos. 9 and 10 are joined on the line by the next in line for the return break.

4. *Pregame Drill:* We have used this one for years, usually the night before a game. It embodies most of the elements of a game and teaches our players to strike on offense immediately or to drop back quickly, find their men, and put on defensive pressure (Diagram 4).

Two teams line up on each side of the center line, with the forwards facing each other and the guards at the foul lines. The coach stands at the side of the center line and throws the ball to a player on one of the teams; the receiving team must go on offense immediately and drive for the basket. The other team is allowed to shoot and rebound for another shot if possible. If the defensive team gets the rebound, they are allowed one fast break down the floor. The coach will alternate throw-ins to give all players opportunities for the offensive thrust.

# 3

## DRILLS TO PERFECT THE FAST BREAK

### by Edwin J. Ryan

*Former Head Basketball Coach*
*Pembroke-Country (Kansas City, Missouri) Day School*

*In Memoriam*

Edwin J. Ryan was the head basketball coach at Pembroke-Country (Kansas City, Missouri) Day School for 12 years. Over the years, his teams compiled an impressive record of 214 wins against only 52 defeats. He never had a losing season at Pembroke. Coach Ryan died suddenly in 1964. This article is reprinted in his memory.

At Pembroke-Country Day School, we start organized basketball at the seventh grade level, with all coaches running the basic offense and defense that we use at the varsity level. Primarily, we use a fast-break offense and a man-to-man defense.

We work very hard in the lower grades on fundamentals. In this way, by the time the boys reach high school level, we do not have to spend a great amount of time on this part of the game.

In the first practice session, we explain how we want the boys to get the ball down the floor—we do not emphasize the long pass, but rather filling the passing lanes and reaching the scoring area with three men at the same time. We use many drills in our practice sessions and very little scrimmage, for we want our boys hungry to play in a game. Here are some of the drills we use to perfect our offense.

*Diagram 1:* Here's how we line up, with our opponents shooting the free throw.

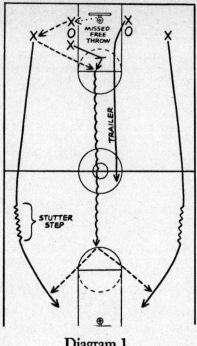

**Diagram 1**

We emphasize that no one runs away from the ball, but that our players should always come to meet the pass. With our two biggest boys lined up in the inside lanes, we put our best ball handler in the cutoff lane. His job is to block out the free thrower and then fill the lane for the outlet pass. If the free throw is missed, our inside men clear the ball with a pass to the side they rebound. Our inside men are told not to go down the floor until they are sure that the ball is not coming to their side and they have received the pass from our rebounder. The outside man, as he receives the ball, attempts to get it into the middle, then he fills the outside lane on his side. The forward on the following side fills the other side, with the man not rebounding the ball becoming the trailer.

NOTE: We tell our middle man that we want the ball picked up at the top of our opponent's free-throw lane. We also want the two outside men to reach the passing and scoring areas at the same time—because one or two defensive men cannot adequately defend all three.

*Diagram 2:* When the free throw is made, we always come down the right side. The rebounder, on the right, takes the ball out-of-bounds and gets it in to the outside forward. The middle man goes to the sidelines, making sure that he receives the pass while still in the back court. The far side

**Diagram 2**

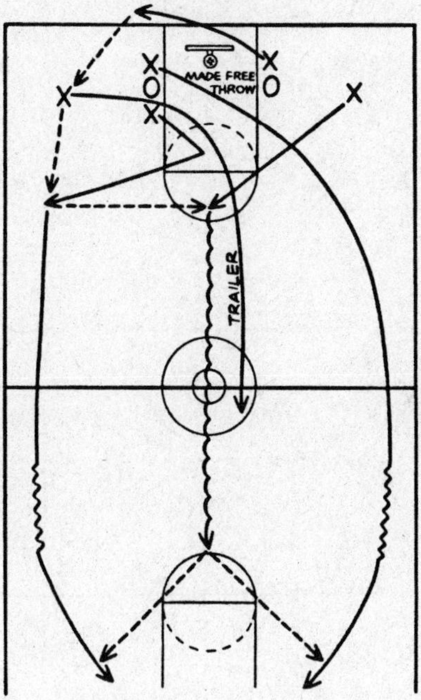

forward fills the middle lane, and the rebounder who did not handle the ball fills the outside lane. This has worked for us year after year.

Diagrams 3 and 4 illustrate our fast-break drill, using the entire squad. This not only provides team conditioning, but practice in passing, defense, rebounding, and shooting.

*Diagram 3*: We divide the entire squad into various spots on the floor. Three players attack two, and they continue working until they have either scored or the defense steals the ball.

**Diagram 3**

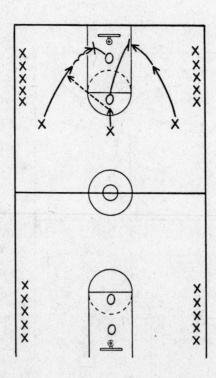

*Diagram 4:* When this happens, there are two men on defense—one of whom throws the ball out to the side, while the other defensive man takes the middle—and they go to the other end of the floor to repeat the process. Three men have come down on the two defensive men now, and the two outside men are the next defensive players—with the middle man and the defensive man who threw the outlet pass going to the outside lines.

**Diagram 4**

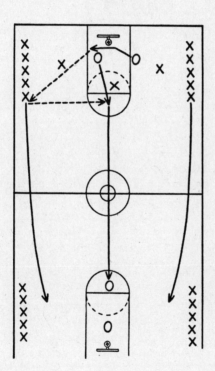

# 4

# FULL-COURT COMPETITIVE FAST-BREAK DRILLS

**by Marion L. Crawley**

*Athletic Director*
*Jefferson (Lafayette, Indiana) High School*

In 1964, Coach Marion Crawley was selected to the Indiana Basketball Hall of Fame—a tribute truly deserved. In 38 years of coaching (27 at Jefferson High School), he has compiled an overall record of 734–231, including 30 sectional tourneys, 20 regional tournaments, 13 semi-state tournaments, and four state championships. Coach Crawley has conducted basketball clinics all over the United States.

One of the most effective ways to improve the fundamental skills connected with the fast break is through the use of full-court continuous action drills which include teamwork, ball handling, timing, and alertness—all learned by the players while moving at top speed.

The use of the full court and the deployment of players on defense in these drills create a teaching situation where the entire squad can get into the action. It is easy for the coach to correct any faulty techniques that show up by stopping the play from time to time to correct mistakes.

The coach should point out time and time again throughout each of these drills that the ball is precious; it must be passed accurately, caught, dribbled, and controlled until a good percentage shot can be made. Wild passes, fumbles, or interceptions must be reduced to a bare minimum if this type of offense is to be of any value.

Here are some of the drills that we use and how we work them:

### THREE-MAN PASS, GO-BEHIND DRILL

This drill has the players pass, dribble, and shoot as they move toward the basket at full speed. It definitely contributes to the development of the fast break. The drill is a standard one, but we have added some spice. As the first player arrives at the basket for a lay-up going under either in a clockwise or counterclockwise direction, the other two reverse immediately and circle toward him in the same direction. They each rebound and pass the ball back until all have taken a lay-up. When they have, they reform and start back toward the opposite basket, following the same procedure as above. If the coach feels that the performance is under par, he can signal repetitions until he is satisfied (Diagram 1).

### FIVE-MAN PASS AND GO-BEHIND TWO DRILL

This drill, too, has been widely used by coaches. However, just as in the preceding drill, we believe we get much greater benefits from it because of the addition of circling, rebounding, and shooting at each basket by all five players. We also get increased player interest because everybody "gets

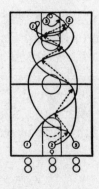

**Diagram 1**

a word in." The only difference between this and the three-man pass, go-behind drill is that five men instead of three are used. Each one passes and goes behind two until arriving at the basket, where one takes an under-the-basket lay-up. When this shot is taken, the other four change and follow in a clockwise or counterclockwise direction, each rebounding and passing back to the next until all have shot and rebounded.

The drill can teach players better timing if they run in a large circle around the area of the free-throw circle. Again, as in the preceding drill, the coach can signal repetitions. Repeating this drill several times takes a great deal of stamina—we have found it to be one of our best conditioners (Diagram 2).

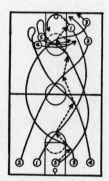

**Diagram 2**

## THREE-ON-TWO, TWO-ON-ONE CONTINUOUS-ACTION DRILL

This is one of our favorite drills and we use it each week throughout the season. It starts by having two lines of players on one end of the court ready to take their turns. Two players are placed on defense at the opposite end, either in tandem (most of the time) or in split formation. In the first movement of the drill, we add an extra man in the middle at the offensive end of the court. The coach tosses the ball against the board, where it is received by the middle man.

The ball is then passed to either side man and the three move down the court to the foul line, where the middle man has the option of shooting or passing to the players on either side. The player who started on offense in the left lane then retreats downcourt with the two original defenders (now on offense), bringing the ball down for the two-on-one situation. This allows the other two original offensive players to remain back as the defense for the next three-on-two maneuver. The drill becomes a continuous three-on-two, two-on-one, with the entire squad working the action. The key to the whole thing is to watch the action of player A. He first starts in the left lane, then retreats by himself on defense against the two original defensive men, picks up these two men, and advances up the court on offense. He remains there with a partner on defense until they get possession of the ball for a two-man drive to the basket, where they both retire to the ends of the lines.

To give players practice in advancing the ball against pressure, we bring the two defensive men up to the front court, where they try to stop the break before it crosses the ten-second line. After this, they retreat close to the basket and take their turn there on defense. This pressure defense causes the offense to adjust and make different moves to be able to work the ball up the floor (Diagram 3).

Diagram 3

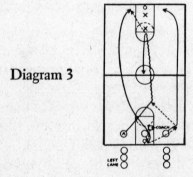

## THREE-ON-TWO CONTINUOUS ACTION DRILL

This drill is started by the coach throwing the ball up against the board, with three players waiting to rebound and break. It is designed to provide a continuous three-on-two situation. A third defensive man works into the play after the three players breaking down the floor have passed the mid-line. He moves in late to help on defense if the two initial defensive players can stall the break temporarily for him to get in position.

When the ball is recovered by one of the players on defense, he starts a fast-break pattern toward the opposite basket along with the other two men. The three players just completing the fast break move off the floor, and one joins the line at midcourt, while the two remaining ones go to the ends of the lines off the floor under the basket (Diagram 4).

The two defensive men may use the tandem formation —one behind the other—or a split defense. This gives the players working against them excellent practice in reacting to the various tactics of the defense.

## THREE-ON-THREE CONTINUOUS-ACTION DRILL
## WITH A TRAILER

This drill brings into play a fourth man as a trailer. Three lines of players are stationed at each end of the court

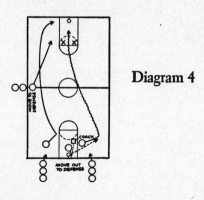

**Diagram 4**

and one line at midcourt. As in the previous drill, the coach
starts the action by throwing the ball up against the board
with three defensive players at the opposite basket. When the
three breaking men pass midcourt, the fourth player comes
on from the side as a trailer. He breaks to either side of the
middle man, looking for a pass. If he gets the ball, he may
shoot from near the foul line or drive on into the basket for a
lay-up. When the middle man is stopped, he may pass to
either side man, then cut on through to clear the floor for
the trailer. When the defense recovers the ball, they break
for the opposite basket, where they will be opposed by three
players who have come from the lines under the basket.
When players have completed their turns, three join the lines
at the end and one goes to the line along the side of the
court (Diagram 5) .

## COMPETITIVE CONTINUOUS-ACTION THREE-ON-ONE DRILL

When a three-on-one fast-break situation comes up,
the numerical advantage should provide a good lay-up shot.
We work on this in this drill. Three lines of players are
formed at each end of the floor. Those in the middle line
become defensive men while those in the two outside lines
become offensive men, making it possible to keep a continu-

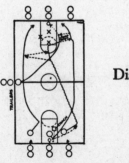

**Diagram 5**

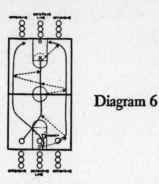

**Diagram 6**

ous three-on-one situation going at all times. Again, the coach throws the ball against the board to start the drill. The middle man rebounds and tosses to one of the side men, cutting toward the sideline. The ball is passed or dribbled to a player in the middle area, where it is advanced by passing not more than once to either side man and back to the middle man, who dribbles to the defensive man. He then fakes with his head and eyes and makes a low bounce pass to either side man for a lay-up shot. To execute this key pass correctly, the player should bend well forward at the waist to be in a position to make a low bounce pass under the arms of the defensive man. At the conclusion of each break, the defensive man recovers the ball and passes out to one of the two players who have just come from the outside lines to a position on the floor, ready to go the moment the ball is captured by the defensive man. The two offensive men who just completed play move to the ends of their respective lines to await their turn again. The defensive position is filled each time by a player from the middle line, who should move up near the center of the floor ready to retreat when opposed by three men breaking toward the goal he is defending (Diagram 6).

# 5

# CONDITIONING DRILLS FOR THE FAST BREAK

## by Bob Fuller

*Head Basketball Coach*
*Elgin (Illinois) High School*

Bob Fuller has been coaching high school basketball for nine years—five years at Chesterton (Indiana) High School, three years at Shabbona (Illinois), and one year at his present post, Elgin (Illinois) High School. His overall record is 195–54 and includes five conference and six tourney championships. This past season he was voted "Coach-of-the-Year" for his area. The following article is based on his work at Chesterton.

Some coaches use the fast break as their entire game plan, fast-breaking every time they have the ball. Others advocate the "ball-control" pattern type of game. At Chesterton High School, we're somewhat in between the two. We always look for the fast break upon gaining possession of the ball, and we always maintain control when the fast break is obviously lost.

Regardless of the degree of the fast break, there are two main objectives desired by the fast-break team: (1) to maneuver the ball from the back court to front court before the defense can get set, getting 3-on-1, 3-on-2, etc. situations; (2) to set up a quick-scoring play without having to develop an offensive pattern.

The fast break, to be successful, must be introduced early in the season and drilled until it is automatic. The fundamentals of passing, dribbling, running, timing, and shooting must be expertly executed. The fast break takes top physical and mental conditioning. We use the following drills to help in this respect.

## 11-MAN DRILL

Figure 1 illustrates our 11-man drill, which we run every day before practice. It's of the continuity type and may continue up and down the floor until you call a halt. The drill involves every fundamental in the book—including the passing, timing, shooting, running, and dribbling previously mentioned.

Figure 1

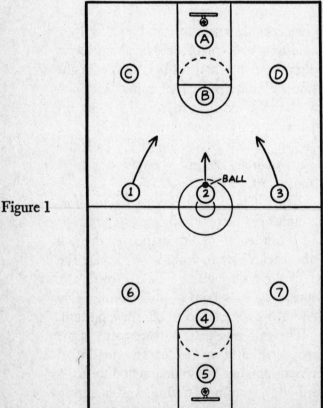

If you have more than 11 boys on your squad, you can alternate the extra boys. Sometimes, we replace one or more of the 11 boys on the floor with an extra boy when they commit errors, fail to hustle, etc.

In the 11-man drill, 1, 2, and 3 take the ball down the floor (2 has the ball). A and B are in the tandem defense for the fast break. B challenges the ball—A takes the first pass— B drops off to the opposite side. When the shot is taken, 1, 2, and 3 and A and B are rebounders. The player that gets the rebound throws out to the side (outlet men) to C or D. For example, A rebounds and then joins C and D in moving to the opposite end of the floor.

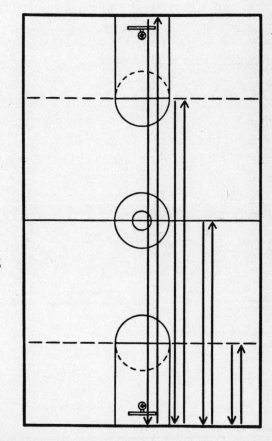

**Figure 2**

B and 1, 2, and 3 fill in the remaining positions—two as the rebound outlet men and two in the defensive tandem. The drill continues up and down the floor until you wish it to subside.

### RUN THE LINES

Figure 2 illustrates our "run the lines" drill (showing the path of one player). On signal, the players (arm's length apart) go full steam to the first free-throw line extended. They touch the floor and then return to their respective original stations. After this, they run to the midcourt line and return; then to the free-throw line extended at the opposite end of the court and return; and finally to the end line at the opposite end and return. The four steps are executed continuously and at full steam. As many repetitions as desired may be run.

For the 1-on-1 full-court drill, we pair off teammates according to ability. Players work the full court. The game may be started by the coach throwing the ball against the backboard or by a jump ball. We play a game of 10 points— 2 points for a basket and 1 point for a steal. A 2-on-2 or 3-on-3 full-court drill can be run using the same rules.

# 6

# THE FAST-BREAK OFFENSE: DRILLS AND IDEAS

**by Bob Macy**

*Head Basketball Coach*
*Indiana Institute (Fort Wayne, Indiana) of Technology*

Bob Macy became head basketball coach at Indiana Institute of Technology in 1960 after a successful high school coaching career (162–70). At Indiana Tech he has posted a 193–92 mark, which includes five conference titles and one NAIA district 21 title.

One of the most effective ways to improve your fast-break offense is through drills which include shooting, passing, rebounding, and ball handling—all at top speed and under pressure. Here are some fast-break drills and ideas that have helped us along these lines. With very minor adjustments, the drills can be applied on either the high school or college level.

## REBOUND-BREAK DRILL

The key to the fast break is the rebounding and initial pass-out to trigger the break. We feel this rebound-break drill (Diagram 1) is of great value since pressure is put on the rebounders at all times. There is also little or no waiting between rebounds; therefore, the endurance is helped. While rebounding is stressed, the break is also utilized by a

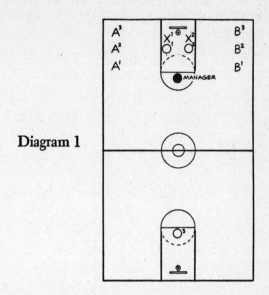

**Diagram 1**

two-on-one situation that is set up. Pressure is on the shooter, since he must go on defense against the next two men on fast break if he misses a shot.

Lines A and B are formed; these are the offensive break men. Two defensive rebounders (X1 and X2) are placed under the basket. O1 and O2 are the pressure rebounders, who attempt to slip inside or knock the ball from the hands of X1 and X2. A student manager is stationed at the foul line to shoot the rebound shots. As soon as X1 or X2 rebound the ball, he passes to the first man in either line A or B. On the first pass-out, A1 or B1 immediately passes back to the manager who shoots again. The rebound and pass-out follow. This time, A1 and B1 fast-break against O3. If a shot is missed by A1 or B1, the shooter replaces O3 on defense.

While the break is on, the manager has another ball in action—and the rebound and pass-out drill is continued. We usually find that the two pass-outs before the break clear the far end so that the danger of congestion is eliminated.

After the fast break, A and B change lines. O1 and O2 are usually kept in the pressure spots as are X1 and X2 until the coach calls for a change.

### FAST-BREAK-CENTER LONG PASS DRILL

The long pass, although sometimes very risky, is nevertheless a definite possibility in the fast break. This drill (Diagram 2) not only helps the center practice his passing, but is also a good conditioner for the entire squad.

Lines A and B face X1, the center, at the far end of the court. The ball can be started in either line A or B. The first pass is to X1 as he comes up to the top of the circle. A1 and B1 go straight down the court and then in a 45° angle. The angle is started where the foul line, if extended, would strike the sideline. X1 tosses off to either A1 or B1. As soon as the shot is taken, A1 and B1 cross and start back up the floor. X1 rebounds the shot and makes the long pass to the moving targets. A2 and B2 wait until A1 and B1 cross their foul line extended—and then put a second ball in action; thus, continuity is maintained.

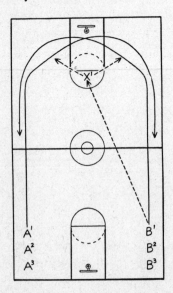

**Diagram 2**

### GO-GO-GO DRILL

This drill is very similar to the Fast-Break-Center Long Pass Drill. However, there is more running involved by all players. The drill gets its name from the fact that the two offensive men must run three hard laps (a lap is considered one length of the floor) each time they are on offense.

As shown in Diagram 3, lines A, B, C, and D are formed. The ball is placed in Line D. D1 long-passes to A1 who moves in the pivot. As soon as either D1 or C1 takes a shot, they then cross and start back up the floor. Meanwhile A1 has rebounded the shot and passes long to B1, who has run to the far-end foul line. B1 receives the pass and can pass off to either D1, C1, or A1 who has become a trailer. D1 and C1 make the third lap, as they must go into A or B line at the far end of the court. A1 and B1 drop into C and D lines. This drill is best used when 12 boys are available.

**Diagram 3**

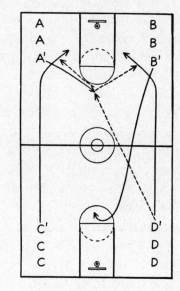

### THREE-ON-TWO FAST-BREAK DRILL

Certainly one of the most common endings to a fast break results in a three-on-two situation. Diagram 4 illustrates a continuity drill that gives three-on-two practice.

Lines A and B are formed on the opposite ends of the court. Both are placed on the right side of their defensive court to avoid confusion. The drill starts with B1, B2, and B3 coming down the floor to attack O1 and O2. As soon as O1 or O2 gets the ball, regardless of whether the shot is made or missed, they then join A1 in a three-on-two fast break towards O3 and O4. O1 and O2 are replaced by A2 and A3 as continuity is maintained. The same action takes place on end B as once again continuity is maintained.

We try to attack the two defensive men (tandem defense) by keeping the three offensive men about 15 feet apart. This allows for speed in ball handling along with safety of passing. No criss-crossing is used since it slows down the penetration. The side men try to get a step or two ahead of the middle man. The center man takes the ball into the defense until he is challenged. He then passes off to either wing man, and they then are in a two-on-one situation to continue the break.

Here a decision must be made whether to stop and jump shoot or drive on in. If we have the size advantage, we usually go on in for 3-point play or the late pass-off. If we are outsized, we shoot the jump shot with the weakside rebounder in good position for the tap-in. The middle man holds his position behind the foul line in case the front man on the tandem retreats fast enough to help cover a man underneath.

Since most teams try to use the tandem defense against the three-man break, we find that usually the smaller man takes the out front position with the taller man under

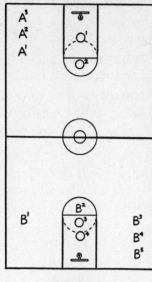
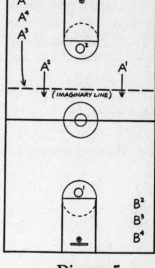

Diagram 4            Diagram 5

the basket for rebound protection. If our middle man out-
sizes the point or out-front man, as soon as the middle man
passes off to a side man, he delays one count, then continues
on in to the basket for a return pass. The point defensive
man usually moves toward the weakside underneath man to
stop a possible pass-off, thus leaving an opening down the
middle of the lane. If the middle man can get the ball back
as he breaks down the lane, he not only has the size advantage
but has the inside position for the driving lay-up. The weakside man comes back to the foul line in case this pass cannot
be made and an outlet is needed.

### TWO-ON-ONE WITH DEFENSIVE TRAILER DRILL

This drill (Diagram 5) speeds up the fast break by
adding a defensive trailer to make sure the two offensive men
don't become lazy or try too many passes.

Lines A and B are formed on the right side of the court at opposite ends. A1 and A2 start a break against O1. As soon as A1 and A2 reach an imaginary line halfway between the top of the circle and the center line, A3 goes on defense as a trailer and tries to help O1. As soon as A3 or O1 gets the ball, whether it is missed or made, he goes on offense on a two-on-one break against O2. B2 waits until O1 and A3 reach the imaginary line; then he becomes the defensive trailer and tries to help O2. B3 takes O1's place on defense as the continuity is maintained.

This drill has the same continuity idea as the three-on-two drill, and is the best drill to use after the three-on-two. Since the boys become tired, they need defensive pressure from behind to keep the break moving at top speed. The boys in the defensive trailer position enjoy trying to catch up and spoil the breaker's advantage.

# 7

# FUNDAMENTALS AND DRILLS FOR THE FAST BREAK

## by Gene Keady

*Head Basketball Coach
Hutchinson (Kansas) Junior College*

Gene Keady has been coaching basketball for the last ten years. His seven-year record as head basketball coach at Beloit (Kansas) High School is 100–46, and includes three trips to the state tournament, two league championships, two league tournament championships, and three regional tournament championships. His three-year record as head basketball coach at Hutchinson (Kansas) Junior College is 65–20. Coach Keady's article is based on his work at Beloit High School.

**O**ur fast break is probably no different than any other fast-break system—except I think we hit better than most small high schools. We have averaged 48% from the field the past three seasons. There are some reasons for this:

1. Our boys take pride in their shooting styles and basketball program.
2. We work on shooting constantly, with shooting drills and fast-break drills (employing shooting in them).
3. Each player has a goal and net in his backyard so he can practice shooting at home.
4. The technique of proper shooting is taught at an early age—the result of a good junior high program.

Next to shooting at a high percentage, the key to a good fast-break team is a tough defense. I don't agree that you automatically have a weak defense when you fast break. You can teach your players to be ball hawks, to steal the ball, rebound, and play an all-around tough defense.

The fast break is not easy to teach in high school; it takes time to teach it right. We spent two years installing it at Beloit High School—but it's been paying off ever since. We installed it for our style of play by stressing the following fundamentals and drills.

### FAST-BREAK FUNDAMENTALS

1. We begin by teaching the location of the lanes—the middle man or lane man always stops at the free-throw line; the two outside lane men go to the 12-inch marks along the free-throw lane; the two trailers split the difference.
2. The fast break depends on quick and accurate passing. Through appropriate drills, our boys learn and master passing on the run.
3. Players are instructed on the proper spacing of lanes— 12 feet. Passes should never be over 12 to 15 feet— unless your man gets behind the defense for the long bomb.
4. We also stress stopping and shooting on the run— usually 10- to 12-foot jump shots.

Most fast-break teams ignore the trailers' part in the game, but they can be most important after your first three men are stopped (Diagram 4).

### FAST-BREAK DRILLS

We have a variety of drills for our fast-break game, covering every situation—and every one has a ball in them. Here are some of our drills.

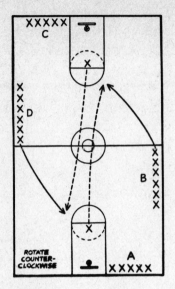

Diagram 1

## Diagram 1—Baseball Pass Drill

In this drill, we use two balls at once. Line A gets one ball and throws it to line B on the right with a baseball pass. Line C gets the second ball out of the basket and throws it to line D on its right. Lines B and D both get the long pass.

## Diagram 2—Two-Lane Fast-Break Drill

Give one ball to each pair of players and have them run down the court passing the ball back and forth at a fast speed—stopping to hit the short jump or lay-up. They get their own rebound and go to the other end.

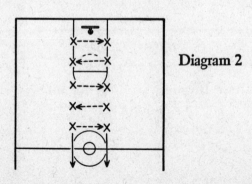

Diagram 2

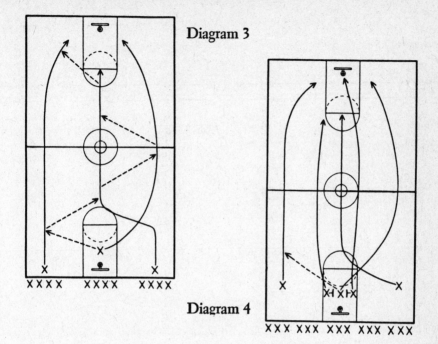

Diagram 3

Diagram 4

### Diagram 3—Three-Lane Fast-Break Drill

Place your centers and big forwards in the middle line; they throw the ball against the backboard, then pass to the outlet man, either side. The side the middle man doesn't pass to breaks to the middle lane; the rebounder or middle man goes the opposite way that he passes out to. Guards and smaller forwards should be in the two outside lanes.

### Diagram 4—Five-Lane Trailer Drill

Here, you add two more lanes; at first they defense the rebounder, but after the middle man gets the pass-off—the two new lanes become the trailers. The right trailer always goes for the lay-up, but the left trailer stays out for the short jumper. You can get screens off this, too.

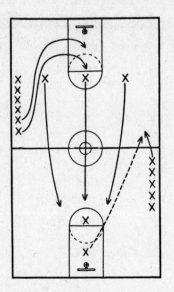

Diagram 5

**Diagram 5—The Blitz**

In this drill, the defense is added. Three men start up the court with two men on defense. As soon as the two defensive men rebound, they pass out to the lead man on their right and have three men breaking back up the court. Now two others have moved in at defense at the opposite end; they rebound and break back up the court with the lead man on their right. This is a good conditioning drill, plus it teaches how to defense a fast break and provides help in practicing your own break, 3-on-2.

# 8

# TWO EFFECTIVE
# FAST-BREAK DRILLS

## by Bob Hendrickson

*Head Basketball Coach*
*Ottawa Hills (Grand Rapids, Michigan) High School*

Bob Hendrickson's eight-year record as head basketball coach at Ottawa Hills (Grand Rapids, Michigan) High School is 127–34 and includes two state crowns, five district and four regional titles, and four city titles.

B esides working on the fundamentals necessary for a good fast break—rebounding, passing, dribbling, and shooting—we stress fast-break drills. Two of our favorites follow.

## PATTERN DRILL

For this drill (Diagrams 1a, 1b, 1c, and 1d), we place five men on the floor and run our fast-break pattern—with the coach shoot-

| Diagram 1a | Diagram 1b |
|:---:|:---:|
| 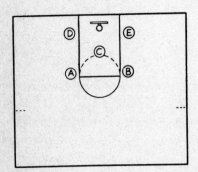 | 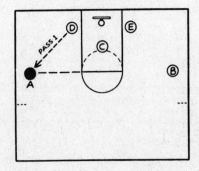 |

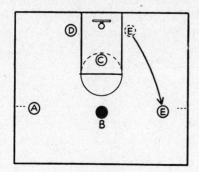

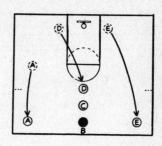

**Diagram 1c**                    **Diagram 1d**

ing the ball each time. During the first week of practice, we
have no defensive players on the floor.

This drill also has value as part of our conditioning
program. After the players run the pattern well with no defense, we then add one and eventually two defensive players.
The defensive players are not used until our boys have confidence in our basic fast-break pattern.

## CONTINUOUS FUNDAMENTALS DRILL

Our continuous drill (Diagrams 2a, 2b, 2c, 2d, 2e, 2f,
and 2g) is well liked by our boys because it is competitive
and combines all the basics of basketball. We run this drill
from ten to 20 minutes each practice session—and twice each
practice during the early part of the season.

The drill begins with a forward or center tossing the
ball against the backboard, rebounding the ball, and passing it
to either guard, who is stationed on either side of the free-
throw line extended (Diagram 2a). The guard receiving the
ball dribbles to the middle of the floor, becoming the middle
man on the break. The other guard fills the outside lane on

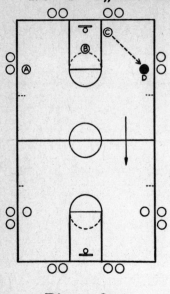

Diagram 2a

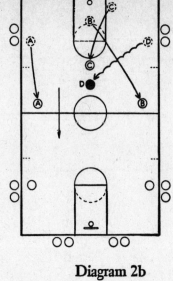

Diagram 2b

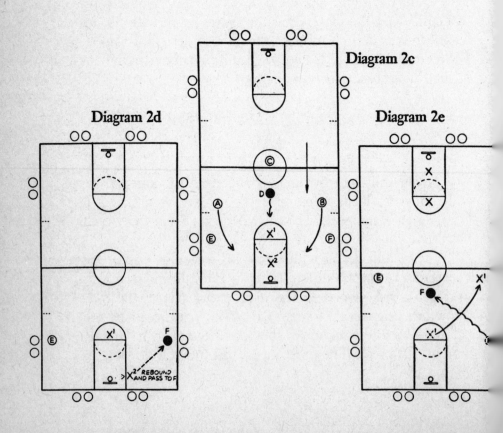

Diagram 2c

Diagram 2d

Diagram 2e

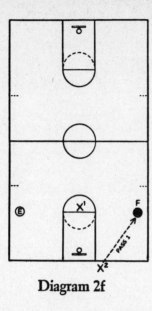

**Diagram 2f**

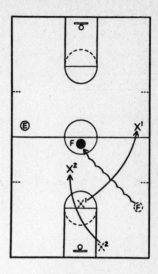

**Diagram 2g**

the side of the floor where he is stationed, while the other lane is filled by one of the other two players. The fourth man becomes the trailer on the play (Diagram 2b). As this group is moving down the floor, two defenders come out to provide the defense against the break (Diagram 2c). These defenders become a part of the offensive group going back down the floor, if the ball is rebounded by them (Diagrams 2d and 2e). If a basket is made, one of the two defensive men grabs the ball, passes to a guard, and again the action is begun (Diagrams 2f and 2g).

The action on a given play continues until a basket is made by the offensive team or until the ball is rebounded by the defensive players.

There is a tendency for the defensive players to get lazy, since they look upon this as an offensive drill. It is important, therefore, for the coach to stress the defensive aspects of the drill as well as the offensive aspects.

# Part III

## DEFENSIVE DRILLS

# 1

# PRESEASON DEFENSIVE DRILLS

## by Michael Cotton

*Head Basketball Coach*
*The Fox Lane (Bedford, New York) Middle School*

Michael Cotton is head basketball coach and teaches physical education at The Fox Lane Middle School of the Bedford, New York public school system. Coach Cotton is prominent in physical education and recreation activities for the New York State Association for Health. His 1970 team won the Class A sectionals in Westchester County.

If good defense is to be employed for an entire ball game, your boys must be in top-flight physical condition. The coach who expects to utilize the full-court, three-quarter court, and half-court presses to maximum advantage must not only prepare his players in the fundamentals of pressure defense—but must see to it that they are physically capable of handling this type of game.

Fox Lane High School in Bedford, New York has built a reputation as a defensive team, and it has helped us to "psych" many opponents. Most teams have respect and a certain fear for a team that is strong defensively —and that little psychological edge can be the difference between winning and losing.

It takes a lot of hard work on your part and on the part of the players, but it's well worth the effort. Of course, your boys must be sold on the fact that there are no shortcuts to hard-nosed defense. Following are some drills and ideas that have helped us build our defensive reputation.

## SUICIDE DRILL

This drill is great for conditioning the total body, but especially the legs. The boys start on the end line, and on the command "go" they sprint to the foul line, touching it with both hands. They then turn and race back to the starting line, touching that with both hands—and then proceed to the midcourt line, the far foul line, and the far end line. After touching these lines the players must go back to the starting line, so that they are racing forward, stopping, turning, and racing back—much like they do in a regular ball game.

This drill can be varied in numerous ways, such as having two boys of equal speed race up and down the court against each other. Also, have the boys dribble a ball and touch with one hand.

## TOE RAISES

This is an excellent drill for strengthening the calf muscles of the leg. The boys line up facing the wall and put their hands against it for support—they then raise one leg up behind them and on the coach's command, "up," they rise up high on their toes. When the coach says, "one," they can lower the foot to the floor. The boys then take over and give the command, "up," while the coach says, "two," etc. until the drill is completed.

We start the boys on 25 toe raises for each foot at the first practice; by the start of the season, they should be able to complete 100 on each foot without stopping.

## MONKEY DRILL

This is a great drill for reaction speed. The squad assumes a defensive position with the knees well bent—while one boy stands in front of the squad and does anything that he wants as fast as he can. The squad must follow his every move.

The leader can do such things as: clap his hands; roll on the floor; simulate a jump shot; jump up and down; run side to side or forward and backward; drop down and execute a fingertip push-up.

There are many things the leader can do—the imagination of the coach and the players is the only limit.

### FOLLOW THE LEADER

This drill is executed with the boys maintaining defensive positions for the entire period. The lines on the court are a guide, and the boys start in a straight line behind the end line of the court. On "go" the first boy races up the sideline to midcourt, then cuts across the midline in a defensive slide, never crossing the feet.

When he hits the other sideline, he races forward to the far end line, and slides the opposite way to the other sideline. The player has now travelled the entire length of the court, and all of the other players have followed close behind. The leader now races backwards down the sideline to midcourt, and then sideways to the other side, and backwards again, until he hits the far end line. At this point, he drops down and executes ten fingertip push-ups, and the rest of the boys follow suit.

### NOSE-TO-NOSE

This drill is for sharpening up on our press. There are two boys working together—one boy on offense with a ball, and the other boy on defense. The defensive man must hold his hands behind his back and stay in front of the offensive man as he zig-zags all over the floor, attempting to get past the defensive man. The players switch positions once they reach the other end of the court and come back the other way.

### ONE-ON-ONE

This is a good, tough drill which we use over the entire court. Two boys of equal size come out and jump center, trying to control the tap and get the ball. They then play fullcourt and everything goes. The ball is never dead and we play up to three baskets at the most.

The loser does a suicide run; the boys are really exhausted after this drill. I keep a record of who wins in this one—and at the end of the year the boy winning the most games receives the "Iron Man" award.

### SUMMARY

These drills have been a big help for us in building good defensive teams. Remember, your boys must first be sold on the importance of defense. Then you can work drills such as these into each practice session with intelligence. Progressively increase the length of each drill, with emphasis on intensity. The drills are virtually useless unless they are executed at maximum effort.

# 2

# DRILLS TO TEACH DEFENSE: A BASIC APPROACH

## by Dean Wilburn

*Head Basketball Coach*
*Harrison (Arkansas) High School*

Dean Wilburn has been coaching high school basketball for 11 years and has an overall record of 330 wins and only 80 losses. In three years at Scranton (Arkansas) High School he posted an 83–25 mark, which included a state runner-up; in three years at Valley Springs (Arkansas) High School, he posted a 105–23 mark which included two conference crowns. At present he is head basketball coach at Harrison High School, where his five-year record is 142–32, and includes four conference championships and one state title.

Since it's our feeling that defense is 75% effort and 25% know-how, we don't spend a great deal of practice time teaching small mannerisms and precise moves to make on defensive plays.

Instead, we try to give the boys a basic foundation of defensive knowledge in the pre-season practices—then we rely almost entirely on drills to do most of the teaching.

Here are some of the defensive drills that have done the job for us.

### ONE-ON-ONE

This one-on-one drill (Diagram 1) is used from five spots on the floor where we figure a defensive boy will most commonly set up in his initial defensive assignment. The offensive player will wait until the defensive player is set; then he fakes a shot, and may take the shot, drive, or use any move that he wants to attempt a shot.

141

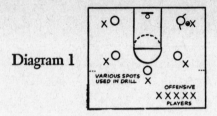

Diagram 1

In this drill, we stress that the defense protect the base line and always turn the offensive player to the inside for help. If we are working on the point, we overplay the individual's strong side.

A defensive player remains on defense until he stops someone from scoring; he then returns to the offensive line. The offensive player goes on defense if he fails to score—but may return to the offensive line if he can score over the defense.

### ONE-ON-ONE WITH POST

Our one-on-one with a post (Diagram 2) is used to teach individual defensive moves. It's the same as the one-on-one, with the exception of the offensive player having a partner in the post man. The post man is allowed to screen for the offense, receive and return passes, or do anything that a normal offensive player can do except shoot and rebound.

Diagram 2

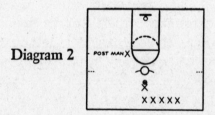

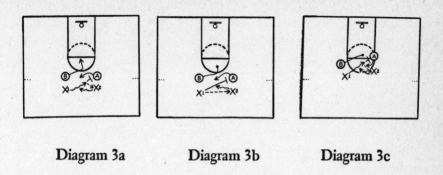

Diagram 3a          Diagram 3b          Diagram 3c

## TWO-ON-TWO

We use a two-on-two drill (Diagrams 3a, 3b, 3c) to teach the defensive players to drop back and allow their buddy player to pass through when the offense is out of the critical scoring area. Also, this teaches them to go over the top of screens or to switch when the offense is in the scoring area. We have the offensive players to exchange or hand-off, pass, and go screen for each other in this drill.

Diagram 3a shows X1 exchanging with X2 and screening defensive player OA. OB goes with X1 until exchange is made, then he moves back to allow OA to move between OB and X1 in pursuit of X2. Diagram 3b illustrates a pass from X1 and X2 and a screen which OA avoids by moving between the screen and defensive player OB, who has dropped back and given him room. Diagram 3c shows X1 and X2 exchanging the part of OA fighting over the screen in the scoring area.

## FIVE-ON-FIVE

We use a five-on-five drill (Diagram 4) to teach the team phase of our man-to-man defense. In this drill we show the players where we want them to play in relation to where

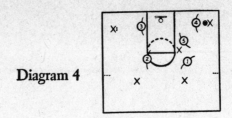

Diagram 4

the ball is and in relation to their man. We place the offensive men in different offensive formations, such as the 1-3-1 or 2-1-2, and simply have them move the ball very slowly so that we can check the defensive alignment.

Note position of defensive players O3 and O2; they should shift as close to the basket as possible, to help in case of a drive or a lone player cutting for a basket. Defensive players O1 and O5 must be more preoccupied with their assignments, because they are in position to receive a direct pass from the offensive player with the ball.

### THREE-ON-TWO

To teach a boy to shift in a zone defense, we use a three-on-two drill as shown in Diagrams 5a and 5b. We start the drill with the offense set up in a triangle in front of the basket with the point player initiating play. The two defensive players are lined up, with one guarding the point man and the other responsible for the other two offensive players.

Diagram 5a                    Diagram 5b

The latter defensive man divides his distance between his two offensive men, so that he may shift to either player to which the ball is passed.

When the ball is passed to a wing, the base-line defensive man covers the wing. Then the point defense drops back midway between the point and the opposite wing, where he is responsible for both of them. The ball is put into free play until the offense scores or the defense stops them.

## DEFENSIVE SLIDES

To teach the defensive slides of a zone defense, we use six offensive men against the zone as shown in Diagrams 6a, 6b, and 6c. We station the six in different offensive sets —and allow the post freedom of movement, and maybe one (sometimes both) corner man to move up and down the base line. The offense moves the ball very slowly at first; each offensive player fakes a pass inside and then passes to the next offensive player.

This permits us to check the defensive slides to see that they are correct. After the slides are perfected, we allow the offense to move the ball rapidly, trying to get off a good shot after eight or ten passes.

### Two-on-One

Our two-on-one drill (Diagram 7) is especially good in developing a pressing type of defense. We set up with an

| Diagram 6a | Diagram 6b | Diagram 6c |
| --- | --- | --- |

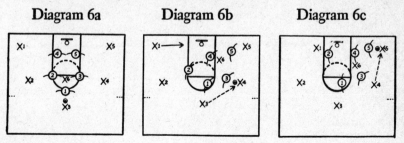

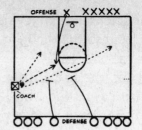

Diagram 7

offensive player under the basket, outside the court, and two defensive players at midcourt. The coach starts the play from the sidelines by rolling or passing the ball onto the court so that the offense can retrieve.

When the coach rolls the ball, it is the signal for the defense to attack; they must stop the offensive player from taking the ball across midcourt without fouling the offensive player.

If the offensive player gets through the defense, the defensive player permitting him to do so is penalized. Both defensive players may be guilty of letting him by and both may be penalized. The penalty holds if the offensive player is fouled. If the defense picks up a charging foul from the offense or forces the offense to make a mistake, then the offense is penalized.

# 3

## DEFENSIVE DRILLING WITHOUT THE BALL

**by Dorsey Sims, Jr.**

*Head Basketball Coach*
*Riverside (Chattanooga, Tennessee) High School*

Dorsey Sims, Jr. took over as head basketball coach at Riverside (Chattanooga, Tennessee) High School in 1965–66—and he has done wonders since then. In his first season he posted a respectable 18–10; his second year was 32–4; his third year was 32–2, which included the state title; his fourth year was 33–0, a second state title and a fourth place rating in the nation; the fifth year was 25–5 with district, region, and sub-state titles; the sixth year was 19–9 —a remarkable six-year record of 154–27.

An observer might liken our defensive drilling to shadow boxing; the players go through the motions, but there isn't any basketball in sight.

That's because we feel that good defense, for the individual and the team, must be based on practice that does not involve the ball.

Our thinking is that the body must acquire specialized skills for defense before ball-handling becomes a factor

### PRACTICE EMPHASIS

Defense was the key to our recent success, and we devote the first three weeks of a five-to-six-week preseason practice to that phase of the game before taking up offense.

We start with conditioning sprints and move to "starts and stops," fundamentally a sound defensive maneuver.

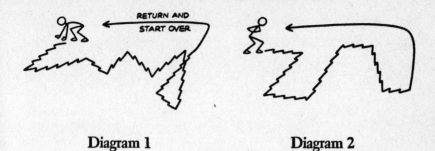

RETURN AND
START OVER

**Diagram 1**                    **Diagram 2**

### PROGRESSIVE DRILLS

From there we move to more positive or progressive drills. The "ape drill" in Diagram 1 tells a coach immediately which players are willing to work on defense, and which just want to play at basketball.

The drill is executed with knees flexed, buttocks down, and palms on the floor. The player then shuffles on hands and balls of feet for as long as ten minutes.

This drill is very demanding, and some coaches also employ it for disciplinary action.

### ANOTHER SHUFFLE

In an upright shuffle (Diagram 2) the knees are in the flexed position of Diagram 1, but the hands are kept idle behind the back.

### MOCK GUARDING

In the next step, the player is allowed to use his hands (Diagram 3) and simulate guarding an opponent as he shuffles eccentrically the length of the court.

Close attention also is paid to footwork and movement of arms and hands to achieve maximum coordination.

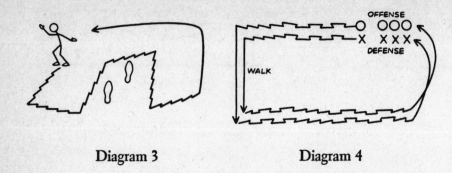

Diagram 3                    Diagram 4

A good stance should be a heel-to-toe relationship, with buttocks low, and one hand up, one down. The player moves in a boxer's shuffle, jabbing at the imaginary basketball with the lower hand.

## USING A CHASER

We take the drill in Diagram 2 and add a chaser. The result may be seen in Diagram 4, which pictures an offensive man and a defensive man with hands behind his back—no ball, of course.

The offensive man makes all kinds of moves up and down the sideline of the court, and the defensive man is supposed to stay with him.

The defensive man must try to play nose-to-nose with the offensive player and never be any more than one-half step behind.

## HANDS PERMITTED

As in Diagram 3, the defensive man in Diagram 5 may use his hands to cover the offensive man. Once again we look for heel-toe stance relationship, hands up, buttocks low, and

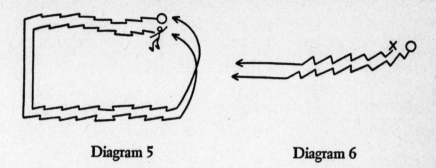

**Diagram 5**          **Diagram 6**

a good boxer's shuffle with lower-hand stab for the imaginary ball.

At the end of these dual drills the boys exchange places, with offense taking on defense's role and defense becoming offense.

### CHANGING DIRECTION

In Diagram 6 there are again offensive and defensive men, with the latter holding hands in back, as in Diagram 2 —but with direction changed from side to side of the court to backwards, and side-to-side stepping.

In Diagram 7 the action is similar, with closer guarding and the defensive man able to use his hands.

### SPEED ACTION

To top off our drills we use the right-and-left wave drill shown in Diagram 8, which calls for speedy action in wide zig-zags down the court.

**Diagram 7**          **Diagram 8**

# 4

# MAN-TO-MAN
# DEFENSE DRILLS

## by Marion L. Crawley

*Athletic Director*
*Jefferson (Lafayette, Indiana) High School*

In 1964, Coach Marion Crawley was selected to the Indiana Basketball Hall of Fame—a tribute truly deserved. In 38 years of coaching (27 at Jefferson High School), he has compiled an overall record of 734–231, including 30 sectional tourneys, 20 regional tournaments, 13 semi-state tournaments, and four state championships. Coach Crawley has conducted basketball clinics all over the United States.

Complete mastery of the fundamentals of man-to-man defense is a long, tedious affair. There is no better way to improve a player's defensive skill than through drills that break the defense down into its different phases. Here are four drills that do the job for us at Jefferson High School.

### FOOTWORK DRILL: (DIAGRAM 1)

Use a stop-watch with this drill. Work ten seconds at a slow warm-up speed. Work 20 seconds at half-speed. Work 30 seconds at full speed. Change the tempo on the coach's whistle. This one minute of continuous action provides an excellent workout.

In guarding without the use of hands, 1 moves to the right, left, then right, changing direction quickly as he works between the end line and the midcourt line. X1 hooks his hands inside his trunks and in good balanced defensive position, attempts to keep in front of 1

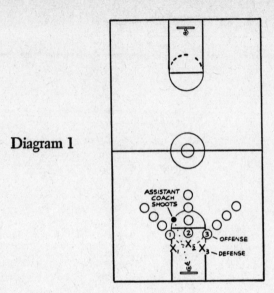

**Diagram 1**

with quick reaction and good footwork. His eyes are kept on the midsection of his man. Follow up, repeating the same drill, except allow the defensive players to use their hands normally.

## MASS REACTION DRILL: (DIAGRAM 2)

The coach uses a stop-watch. Each player keeps his right hand up for one minute, followed by the left hand for one minute, to develop endurance. This drill takes a lot of room.

The squad spreads out along one side of the court. One player with a ball faces the group. While he dribbles, changing direction from right to left, forward and backward,

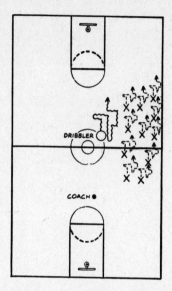

Diagram 2

they react to his move with correct footwork, using an approach step, retreat step, and side step.

## REBOUND DRILL: (DIAGRAM 3)

Arrange the players in three lines. The assistant coach throws the ball above the basket, trying to miss the shot. The coach watches each player as they screen out their men, turn, and go for the ball.

X1, X2, and X3 rotate, each taking three turns before going to the end of the line. The next three players move from offense to defense. Offensive players should be instructed to make a good effort to follow in to give the defensive rebounders a good workout. Two players can be placed out near the sidelines on either side to receive a pass-out from the defensive rebounder.

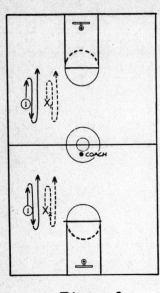

Diagram 3

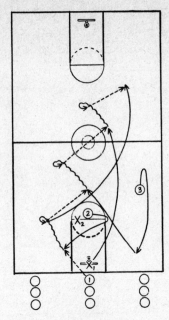

Diagram 4

## THREE-ON-THREE FULL-COURT DRILL: (DIAGRAM 4)

After players have worked on the one-on-one and two-on-two, they are then ready for one of the most effective drills to teach man-to-man fundamentals. The squad forms three lines. One man from each line steps on the court and assumes a defensive position.

1 starts the drill by passing in to 2, who uses a change of direction out to break into the clear for the pass. 3 breaks up the floor, then returns, ready to get the pass in if 2 cannot shake his man. No player is allowed to break all the way to the opposite end for a long pass. Once the ball is on the court, it is advanced by passing, screening, dribbling, and cutting off each other. If a player with the ball gets into the

clear, he dribbles only a short distance, stops, pivots, and passes, allowing the defense to reform. This offers the defense a real challenge all the way. Following a basket or recovery of the ball off the board by the defense, positions are reversed before starting back. Switch players around so that big men have the opportunity to guard small men and vice versa.

# 5

## PRESSING
## MAN-FOR-MAN DRILLS

**by Lofton Greene**

*Athletic Director*
*River Rouge (Michigan) High School*

In 25 years at River Rouge (Michigan) High School, Lofton Greene has put together a career record of 500 wins and only 103 losses. And during that time, he has seen his share of conference, district, and state titles. Coach Greene is athletic director as well as head basketball coach at River Rouge.

Our full-time use of the man-for-man press demands top physical condition in the players. Almost all of our drills, therefore, are designed not only to teach the fundamentals of the press but also to help condition the players.

We have five of them that are the basis for our success in coaching the man-for-man press.

## MILITARY DRILL

This drill is one of two we have to prepare the squad for our defense. The squad lines up in three parallel rows arm's length apart, facing the coach. On command, each player assumes the defensive stance and slides according to four commands: "forward," "back," "left," "right." The drill is repeated daily and the length of time is increased each day (Diagram 1).

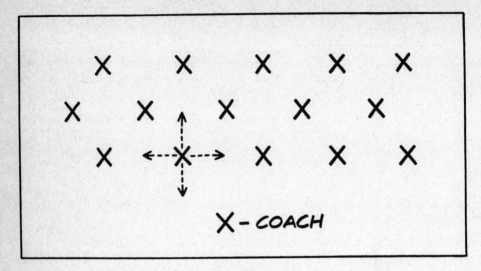

**Diagram 1**

## BULL IN THE RING

This is our second preparatory drill. Six players are stationed equidistant around either of the free-throw circles, with one player in possession of the ball. A defensive player is stationed inside the circle to chase the ball. The player with the ball may not pass to the person immediately on his left or right. The defensive player, utilizing fast footwork, attempts to stay with the ball and tries to steal, intercept, or deflect. On command, another player goes into the ring. The drill is excellent in developing fast footwork in all directions (Diagram 2).

## ONE-ON-ONE

This is our best drill for teaching the man-for-man press. The squad is divided into pairs according to size and

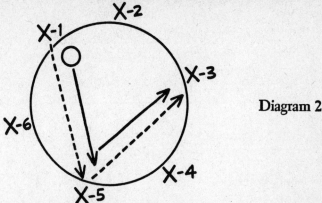

Diagram 2

speed. *Three pairs are going at the same time.* One player takes the ball and attempts to dribble the full length of the court to score. The player on defense guards the entire length of the court very closely and tries to dominate by overplaying one hand, harassing, talking to his opponent, and so on. With three pairs going at once, peripheral vision is employed to avoid player collision. The players exchange on offense and defense and return to the other end of the court (Diagram 3).

### TWO-ON-TWO

In this drill we permit our guards to switch on defense, but we have our forwards and centers stay with their assigned opponent. We generally have the guards work against guards and forwards against forwards. In Diagram 4, X-1 and X-2 are on offense and O-1 and O-2 are on defense. When our guards switch, we want it done aggressively. For example: X-1 passes to X-2, cutting to one side. O-2 should anticipate a switch situation and jump out in front of X-1, coming around for a possible return pass. O-1 should immediately react and get a defensive position on X-2, so he does not get away loose down the floor.

Since we do not permit our forwards and centers to switch, the defense is a little different. If the offensive players

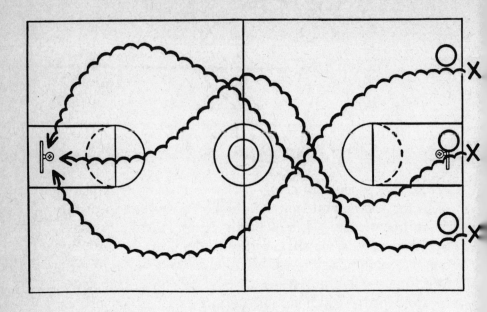

Diagram 3

Diagram 4

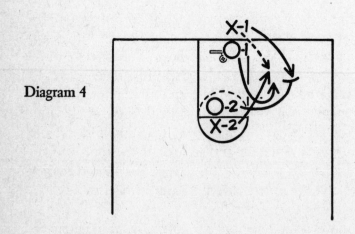

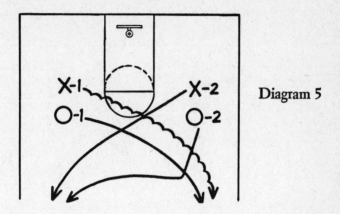

Diagram 5

cross as they advance down the court, the defensive man on the ball plays tight; the other defensive player releases and slides behind his teammate to keep defensive position on his opponent (Diagram 5).

When the offensive pair gets a shot, they go on defense and the other pair attempts to advance the ball to the other basket.

## BIG MAN DRILL

In the man-for-man press, all five players must do a good job; if one or more players loaf, the opponents will spot the weakness. We find that sometimes our big men become lax on defense; to correct this we improvised a special drill (Diagram 6). We station three players around the ten-second line and they can operate any way they see fit to break open for a pass. One of our guards will stand behind the end line with another guard on defense. The guard will attempt to pass the ball to one of the big men breaking back. This

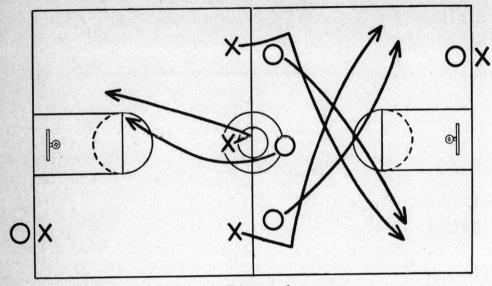

**Diagram 6**

drill helps our forwards and centers to defend against long passes. You can get more mileage out of the drill by having another guard and defensive man at the other end of the court, and alternate passes and offensive and defensive players.

The final phase of developing the man-for-man press is a game-situation drill. We place our team in normal offensive positions, with a defensive team guarding them. I shoot the ball so it will fall out-of-bounds. Our team is to go immediately on defense until they secure the ball or the other team scores. At this point, we repeat the drill.

Everything about the man-for-man press is work, but we feel the results have been worth the effort. All coaches know there are some nights when your players can't seem to make a basket. We depend on our man-for-man press to keep us in the game on those nights.

# 6

# DRILL FOR TEACHING THE ZONE PRESS

**by Ross Shaw**

*Head Basketball Coach*
*Bridge Creek (Blanchard, Oklahoma) Public School*

Ross Shaw has been coaching basketball for 22 years in Texas, Nebraska, and Oklahoma high schools. His overall record is an impressive 263–60. At present, he is head basketball coach at Bridge Creek Public School.

**H**ere's an extremely effective drill for teaching any type of zone press; we call it the "three men in the circle drill." It's just like the old "bull in the ring drill," with the exception that three men are used in the circle —one as an interceptor and two for the double-team. Here's how it works:

Arrange seven or eight players in a circle (Diagram 1). The coach throws the ball to No. ①. Immediately, ①and ②cover him. No. ③ is the interceptor. No. ① makes a successful pass to ⑤ and ① and ③ cover him. No. ② becomes the interceptor.

No. ⑤ passes successfully to ⑧. ② and ① cover. ③, the farthest from the ball, becomes the interceptor (Diagram 2). When the interceptor gets the ball, the man who made the pass must take his place. The two men who double-team do not try to get the ball—they merely try to force a bad pass. Players around the circle cannot pass to the

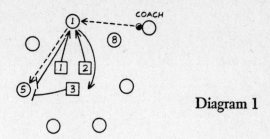

Diagram 1

Diagram 2

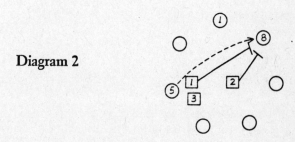

man nearest them—but must pass across the circle.

Emphasize footwork—when double-teaming, the men take sliding steps; the last two steps are toward the ball. Also check for correct body position, balance, heels off floor, arms and hands relaxed, and watching the ball handler to tip off the direction of his pass.

This drill is an excellent conditioner, and it prepares your team for executing the zone press without continual scrimmage. Mistakes can be more easily corrected than in actual scrimmage.

The size of the circle can be enlarged as the players become more effective. We use the center circle of the court at first, then move the players back as the middle men improve.

# 7

# DEFENSIVE THREE-MAN WEAVE DRILLS

## by Herb Robinson

*Head Basketball Coach*
*Presbyterian (Clinton, South Carolina) College*

Herb Robinson has been coaching basketball since 1957. In eight years as head basketball coach at Dreher (Columbia, South Carolina) he posted a 125–28 record with two state championships and one regional title. In three years as head basketball coach at Spartanburg (South Carolina) High School, he compiled a 65–11 mark with one state title and one regional title. At present, he is head basketball coach at Presbyterian College. This article is based on his work at Dreher High School.

I believe that our defensive three-man weave is one of the finest of all defensive drills, and it can be used for offensive and defensive purposes at the same time. The offensive men simply run a three-quarter-speed weave with each defensive man concentrating on stance, position, and movement (Diagrams 1a-1c).

These rules govern our use of this drill:

1. The man guarding the ball always has priority; he has the right of way (Diagram 1a).
2. The man not guarding the ball must open up or be in position to let the priority man through (Diagram 1b). Thus, $X^1$ opens up for $X^2$ and becomes the priority man in Diagram 1c.

The position of the men will vary as to the position of the ball and basket. Each defensive man must not switch, but learn to fight his way through. You can teach the reverse pivot out of a screen in other drills.

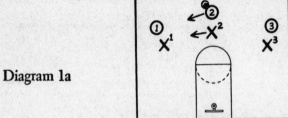

Diagram 1a

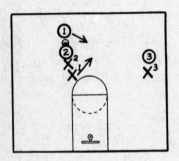

Diagram 1b

Diagram 1c

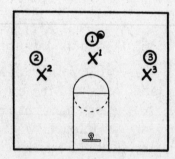

# 8

# DEFENSE:
# DESIRE, DISCIPLINE, DRILLS

by Dick Campbell

*Head Basketball Coach*
*Xavier (Cincinnati, Ohio) University*

Dick Campbell has been coaching college basketball for 18 years and has an overall record of 418–144. At North Greenville (Tigerville, South Carolina) Junior College, he posted a 135–29 mark; at Carson-Newman (Tennessee) College, he posted a 227–64 mark which included five conference titles, two conference tournaments, three NAIA District 27 titles, and five trips to the NAIA national tournament; at The Citadel (Charleston, South Carolina) his mark was 46–51. At present, he is head basketball coach at Xavier (Cincinnati, Ohio) University. The following article is based on his work at Carson-Newman.

At Carson-Newman we basically play man-to-man defense, but with variations: sometimes pressure, sometimes sloughing. We sprinkle in zones if it fits our opposition. Sometimes we mix zones, man-to-man, and presses. We call our defense a Kamikaze Defense, because we put the job ahead of ourselves.

I won't try to tell you how to play defense. I am convinced that defense is the key to success; we changed from a good club to a championship club when we began to place prime emphasis on defense. I think these elements are the basis of a successful defensive team.

## DESIRE

The boys have to *want* to play defense, and this runs counter to natural instinct, which is offense and shooting. The coach, therefore, must be convinced of defense himself and sell

172

it to the boys. Here are some things to build up this desire:

a. At our first squad meeting, we talk mostly about defense and set our goal for the season. I let the players set this target; if it is their choice, they will work harder to achieve it and have the necessary desire.
b. We tell the boys that defense is 90% desire and 10% fundamentals; the ratio may be high, but it helps impress the importance of desire.
c. Our most coveted award at the end of the season is the best defensive player trophy. I believe that every boy on our squad would rather win this than any other award.
d. The boys know that if they can't or won't play defense, they will spend most of the season on the bench.

After a game or two, and the players can see the results, some of the problems are over. Players, students, fans, and the papers will pick up what you are trying to do and will help carry the ball.

## DISCIPLINE

I am convinced that unless you discipline your offense, you cannot have a great defensive team. We tell our boys that they must get the good percentage shot every time they get the ball; it is an unpardonable sin to make a bad pass, travel, double-dribble, palm the ball, or take a poor percentage shot.

## DRILLS

I am sure that many players do not play sound defense because of lack of desire, but because they are not in condition to maneuver like a good defense man should. Check up on your own drills. How many of them require the player to run backward instead of forward, laterally or at an angle, with his back to the basket?

So, at the beginning of practice, we put the ball on the rack and go to work on individual defense. Here are a few of our drills:

    a. *Back Up:* Each player takes his defensive stance and backs up as fast as he can while maintaining good balance and proper defensive position (Diagram 1).

    b. *Oblique:* The players take a defensive stance and move obliquely, using a slide step, being careful not to cross the feet. The second man begins when the first man gets to the top of the circle (Diagram 2).

    c. *Lateral:* The players take a defensive stance facing the coach and move laterally across the floor, using the slide step. The coach can change direction by using the whistle (Diagram 3).

    d. *Combination:* The players take a defensive stance, and on a hand signal from the coach they move backwards, obliquely and laterally, until they have covered the court (Diagram 4).

Diagram 1              Diagram 2

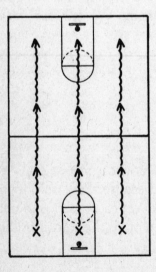
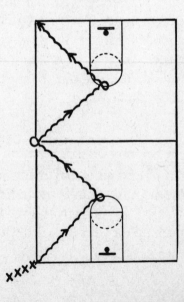

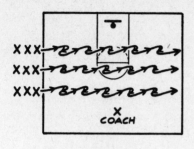

Diagram 3

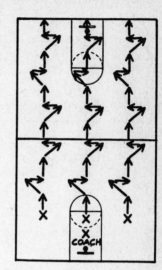

Diagram 4

Later we begin work on our 1-on-1, 2-on-2, 3-on-3, and 4-on-4 defensive drills.

e. *1-on-1:* I believe the 1-on-1, half or full court, is the best way to teach a boy sound individual defense. It is one of the finest drills I know: Each boy is on his own. Offensive man O with the ball tries to score on defensive man D. D tries to stop O's dribble and prevent the shot (Diagram 5).

f. *2-on-2:* In the 2-on-2, we begin to work on the switch and slide-through and usually run this drill full court with automatic switching in the back court (Diagram 6).

g. *3-on-3:* Our 3-on-3 is usually full court, and we tell our boys to switch automatically in the back court. We also begin to teach the boys to look for the double-team situation (Diagram 7).

h. *4-on-4:* Our 4-on-4 is usually half-court, and here we teach switching, sliding through, double-teaming, looking for blind picks, and how to defense the four-man weave (Diagram 8).

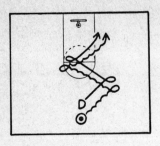

Diagram 5

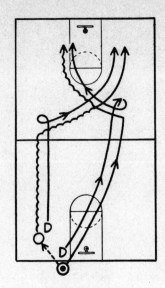

Diagram 6

Diagram 7

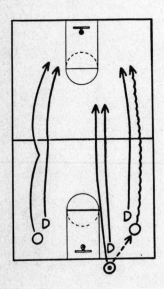

Diagram 8

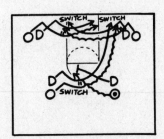

The real purpose of our defense is to force the opponent to do things he doesn't want to do. For example, if a defensive guard likes to go right, we try to force him to go left. If a team starts its patterns with a guard-to-forward pass, we overplay the forwards and the passing guard. If our opponents don't play well when picked up tight, our guards go to get them at midcourt and everyone puts pressure on his man.

# 9

# SPECIAL-PURPOSE DRILLS: DEFENSE

## by Duane Woltzen

*Head Basketball Coach*
*Lakeland (Sheboygan, Wisconsin) College*

Duane Woltzen has been head basketball coach at Lakeland College since 1964. His record is a phenomenal 146–45 and includes seven consecutive conference championships and post-season tourney bids in each of those seven years. He has twice coached all-star teams which have successfully toured Europe in the summers of 1969 and 1971.

eaching defense to an offensive-minded team (over-100-points-per-game average in 79 games) is a difficult task. We know that our players enjoy shooting more than they do playing defense.

With this in mind, we stress the many scoring opportunities that can be had through aggressive defensive play. Because we use the "run and gun" style of play, it's important that we control the tempo of the game. We want our opponents to run with us and to aid us in speeding up play. We utilize pressure-type defenses almost entirely.

Here are some of the drills we use to serve our special purposes.

## 2-ON-2 PLUS THE POST

This drill helps teach the defense to watch the man and not the ball. It also aids in teaching how to defense the split and shows how important it is to talk on defense.

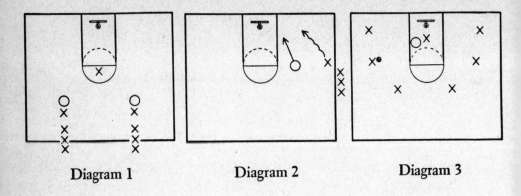

**Diagram 1**          **Diagram 2**          **Diagram 3**

Set up as shown in Diagram 1. The post man cannot shoot but can be used as a screen, an outlet pass receiver, and a passer. The defensive men stay on defense until they steal the ball or stop the offense from scoring in some way. The defensive men go to the end of the offensive line, and the offensive men become the defenders.

### 1-ON-1 PROTECT THE BASE LINE

We purposely put the defensive man in poor defensive position in this drill (Diagram 2) to encourage the offensive man to drive the base line. The defender must use good footwork and take the correct angle of pursuit to cut the offensive man off at the base line. We encourage the defender to put one foot on the end line or out-of-bounds, to stop the drive and force him to pick up his dribble or reverse.

### GUARDING THE POST

This drill puts a defensive man on a post man. The offensive men spread themselves in a semicircle around the keyhole (Diagram 3). They pass the ball around the key, forcing the defensive man to move in order to front the post man.

If the post man gets the ball, he then goes 1-on-1 until he scores or the defender gets the ball. Players then rotate with the offensive post man going on defense and the defensive man becoming a feeder.

## GETTING BACK ON DEFENSE

In this drill (Diagram 4), the offensive team runs a regular pattern. The coach stands at midcourt with an extra ball. When the coach blows his whistle, the offense drops the ball and hustles back on defense. The defense becomes the offense and tries to get the fast break. The coach feeds the open man. The same procedure is followed at the other end of the court.

This drill helps teach the defense to make the transition to offense quickly—and it makes the offense conscious of the importance of getting back on defense in a hurry.

## CHECKING OUT

This drill is set up as shown in Diagram 5. The offense shoots a jump shot. The defensive man guarding the shooter must yell "Shot." The three defenders check the offensive men from the boards and then go for the rebound. Offensive men go on defense and the defenders go to the rear of the offensive lines.

## MULTIPURPOSE DRILL

Our multipurpose drill (Diagram 6) is used to teach various defensive fundamentals. We use only four offensive men because this permits the offense to move more easily— and at the same time it puts more pressure on the defense.

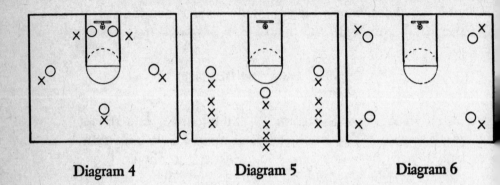

**Diagram 4**          **Diagram 5**          **Diagram 6**

We tell the offense what to do at the beginning of this drill. We find that most offenses do one of the following:

1. Pass and go inside of the man you pass to.
2. Pass and go outside of the man you pass to.
3. Pass and cut for the basket.
4. Pass and set a screen for the man you pass to.
5. Pass and screen for the man away from the ball.

We spend two minutes on each of these situations and then switch the offense and defense. You can also permit the offense to utilize any of the situations they care to.

# 10

## DRILLS FOR TEACHING MAN-TO-MAN DEFENSE

**by Larry Lindquist**

*Ex-Head Basketball Coach*
*Holstein (Nebraska) High School*

Larry Lindquist was head basketball coach at Holstein
(Nebraska) High School. When he took over as
coach there, the basketball team was in a rebuilding
stage. Said Coach Lindquist ". . . Since we started
playing a stronger man-to-man defense (the drills
played a big part), we did better . . . our reserves,
using this defense exclusively, had a .500 season—
and these boys were freshmen and inexperienced."
At this writing, he is the principal at Republican Valleys
Schools, Indianola, Nebraska. This article is based on
his work at Holstein High School.

We run drills for five to seven minutes each and change drills to keep interest high. We have found that boys can help modify drills and really improve them.

No drill is too complicated, but we still feel they should not be run for any extended length any one day because the boys fail to learn when fatigue and boredom set in.

The drills used are always open to amendment from any interested source and are incorporated into the routine after the season begins.

## MAIN DRILLS

We make an effort to keep drills as simple as possible, consistent with proper development, because young athletes respond better to simplicity. The main drills are ten in number.

(1) *Flag Drill:* The squad is divided in

two, with one-half at each end of the floor under a manager or coach. This director points direction (flags) on the ground and the group moves that way until redirected. The coach or manager observes closely for poor stance and crossing of feet while the players are shuffling.

(2) *Wave Drill:* This is a similar drill to the flag drill, but the squad is divided into smaller segments and each segment follows a leader. We make a point of having every boy take a turn leading.

(3) *Stance Run Drill:* Sprints are run from the defensive stance, with knees bent and hands set, with one hand up and one down, to acquire form.

(4) *One-on-One Shuffle:* This drill puts one-on-one; they are to move around the floor in pairs, one on the offensive, the other on the defensive. When we have five groups all moving together on the floor, we feel we are learning about screens also.

We emphasize all our rules in this drill and require our defensive men to be lifting one hand up as if under the ball, to maintain a constant threat to steal it.

(5) *Body Guard Drill:* This is similar to drill 4, but each defensive man must keep his hands behind him and still guard his man to the fullest extent possible.

The drill is designed to improve speed and reaction and aid the defense of a man in foul trouble. It develops the thinking of the boy as to how he can get between his man and the basket the very quickest. We stress that to allow an open shot under the basket is a "cardinal sin."

(6) *Two-on-Two Strict Cover:* This implies just what its name states. Two men pair on two men and no switch is allowed, in a supervised drill of defensive technique.

If boredom interjects itself in this drill (or any other), the squad is allowed to play a half-court game to renew interest.

(7) *Two-Two Switch:* This is the two-on-two strict

cover drill with switching allowed, the main idea being to show when switching is advisable. Talking it up enters this drill, with the defensive men communicating steadily so that they will know how in action.

(8) *Flying Chair Drill:* An obstacle course of chairs is prepared and the team sent through it in defensive stance, forward and then backward.

Forward drill should stress speed and backward drill should stress reaction and adaptation.

Going through backwards, feeling the chairs, can be tough at first. If the coach feels the drill is too dangerous, squad members may be substituted for chairs.

(9) *Hands Down Drill:* This drill can put as many on as many as the coach wishes. It is a half-court drill with defensive men following their offensive counterparts, at the same time feeling for screens.

We have defensive players put one hand backward 6 inches to 1 foot, to contact a screen. Fast footwork must be applied when a screen is felt.

(10) *Footwork Drills:* These maneuvers are planned to develop reaction to keep pace with an open man, to keep with a man coming off a screen, and to pick up a switch in a quick change of direction when a teammate requests it. We find our biggest problem is to get the boys to think quickly on spot situations.

For mobility, from time to time in these drills, we have the team in groups running stance springs, doing front turns, rear turns, and reverse full pivots on whistle signals.

# Part IV

## COMBINATION DRILLS

# 1

# DRILLS FOR SPEED AND PRESSURE

## by Leo M. Smith

*Head Basketball Coach
Robert W. Traip (Kittery, Maine) Academy*

Leo M. Smith is head basketball coach at Robert W. Traip Academy in Kittery, Maine. His five-year record there is as follows: 13–5 (1966–67); 19–1 (1967–68) with a Western Maine championship and a state championship; 19–4 (1968–69); 16–6 (1969–70); 18–5 (1970–71) with a league and Christmas tournament title.

**W**e press on defense and run on offense, and our drills are geared high to support that kind of program. Our drills keep the team running in order to build up stamina to sustain a hot pace for the entire game.

### RUNNING DRILL

Our practice opens with 15 laps around the gym, or fewer laps if we are coming off a hard game or late night travel. Each player as he runs keeps arms extended horizontally at shoulder level.

Speed and arm position are varied on commands by the coach. The idea is to strengthen the upper arms and shoulder girdle as well as the legs, to play a tough defense and strong offense.

### PASS-AND-SHOOT DRILL

Accuracy, controlled speed, and endurance are the goals in our pass-and-shoot drill.

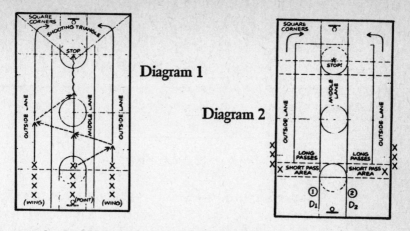

Diagram 1

Diagram 2

It is simply the three-lane passing drill started at three-quarter court with the basic approach to the fast break (Diagram 1).

It is also the familiar point-to-wing passing drill down-court to the shooting triangle. We stress speed but demand that it be controlled for proper execution. If the lay-up is missed, the ball is rebounded until put in the hoop. The next point man gets the ball on a three-quarter-court pass.

### 2-ON-2 FAST-BREAK DRILL

Two offense and two defense men are matched as closely as possible in our 2-on-2 fast-break drill. I try to simulate a game situation, in which our zone press calls on boys to work in pairs or be able to complement each other's coverage. This drill enables them to appraise the strengths and weaknesses of teammates (Diagram 2).

The defensive player must be aggressive in coverage, switch when necessary, block out after the shot, rebound, and clear the ball to the side court to start the fast break.

The offensive player must attack strongly, screen when necessary, work into good shooting position, and work the offensive boards after a shot, trying for control of the rebound.

When the clear-out pass comes up, the men on the sidelines move out to meet it and break the ball downcourt to complete another offensive maneuver. We will combine this drill with a 3-on-2 situation.

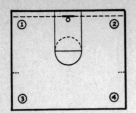
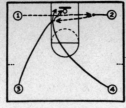
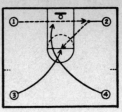

| Diagram 3 | Diagram 4 | Diagram 5 |

## FOUR CORNERS DRILL

We station four lines of players at the four corners of the offensive end of the court (Diagram 3). The No. 1 line is for passing; No. 2 for feeding; No. 3 for shooting; No. 4 for rebounding. The players rotate after their turn, with No. 1 going into the No. 2 line, and so on.

Off this alignment we practice many maneuvers. In Diagram 4 the lay-up is practiced, with No. 1 passing to No. 2, who feeds to No. 3 cutting for the basket. No. 4 follows to play a rebound.

The drill is changed to a jump-shooting practice by having the shooter (No. 3) approach the basket through the top of the key and receive the feed from No. 2 at the top of the foul line (Diagram 5).

A different technique by No. 2 is called for in Diagram 6, for the screen shot. Instead of passing in turn after receiving the ball from No. 1, No. 2 dribbles to the foul line to set the screen.

The fourth move in the four-corner drill calls for a scissoring off the post (Diagram 7), with a resulting handoff and drive down the lane by the shooter (No. 3). A second pass may be inserted to give No. 4 the chance for a drive, jump, or bank shot.

Diagram 6

Diagram 7

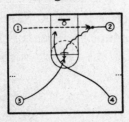
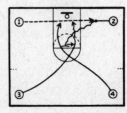

# 2

# DRILLS FOR TEAMWORK

## by Tommy Foster

*Head Basketball Coach*
*West Fannin (Blue Ridge, Georgia) High School*

As head basketball coach at West Fannin High
School, Tommy Foster's 11-year record stands at 201
wins against 94 losses—it includes two regional championships and six teams in the state tournament.

In too many high school basketball games, one or two boys do all the shooting and the others are there just to fill out the team. We believe that a boy will give more overall effort, if he knows that he's a working part of the offense and is given the opportunity to take shots throughout the course of a game. Within reason, we give every boy a chance to be a star.

Drills, the right kind, can be of vital importance in building teamwork. When two or more players work against another group, and success is achieved by one group while the other has to run sprints or something of this nature—competition and teamwork are extended to a high degree.

Here are some of the drills we use to develop teamwork for our continuous shuffle-style offense·

## 3-ON-2

Place three offensive players against two

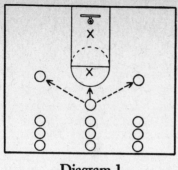
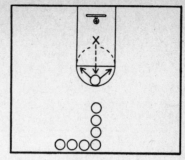

| Diagram 1 | Diagram 2 |

defensive players (Diagram 1). Set up a time limit for the offense to score—then move up three other offensive players. The two defensive players who do the best job are recognized and rewarded—no sprints, for instance.

### GUARD THE LINE

Under the basket at one end of the floor, place a player on defense and the others on offense. The defense takes the ball with his back to the goal and positions himself at the edge of the circle at the free-throw line; the offensive player takes a position at the head of the circle facing the goal (Diagram 2). The defensive player passes to the offensive player and tries to keep him from scoring. If he stops the offensive player, he moves on offense; if he does not, he stays on defense. When the defensive player stops the offense, the next offensive player in the line coming up takes the defense.

For variety we split up the players into groups of two, and each group plays another once. Or, once or twice during the season, we let the squad divide themselves into two teams and play a regulation game. These group and team tournaments provide plenty of competition for the boys, and they work extra hard to compile the best records

### PASSING DRILLS

Good ball handling is most important in our shuffle

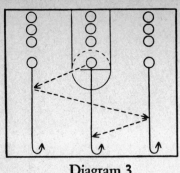

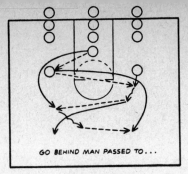

GO BEHIND MAN PASSED TO...

Diagram 3                          Diagram 4

offense, so we stress quite a few passing drills. Here are three of our favorites:

1. *Three lines down the floor*—Players form three lines (Diagram 3) and go down the floor to the end and back, making as many passes as possible. You can run this drill both half-court and full court.
2. *Figure-eight*—Players go the length of the floor (half-court or full court) and back in figure-eight design, making as many passes as possible. Note that each man goes behind the man he passes to (Diagram 4).
3. *Two lines down the floor*—Players form two lines about 10 to 12 feet apart (Diagram 5) and go the length of the floor (half-court or full court) and back, making as many passes as possible.

Accuracy is the important teaching point in all our passing drills.

## LAY-UP DRILL

As part of our game warm-up practice, we do a three-

Diagram 5                          Diagram 6

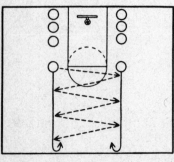

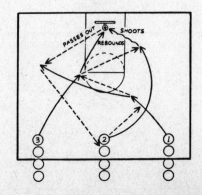

line lay-up drill that employs several phases of basketball (Diagram 6). Starting at half-court, three lines are formed: (1) to the right; (2) in the middle; (3) to the left. Each player moves from 1 to 2 to 3 and back to 1. As the first player in line 2 passes to the first player in line 1, he breaks behind him toward the basket. No. 1 passes to 3, who has gone to the edge of the free-throw line. No. 1 continues to the side of the floor and No. 3 passes to 2, who shoots a lay-up. No. 3 then rebounds and passes to the side of the floor to No. 1, who passes back to the next man in line 2.

This drill perfects passing, shooting, rebounding, timing, and passing out as if a fast-break attack would start.

### HUSTLE DRILL

For the hustle drill, we divide the squad in half and place one group at each end of the floor. Three players start down the floor for a 3-on-2 attack (Diagram 7). The two players on defense will go toward the other end of the floor, with one more player out of the group after they stop or fail

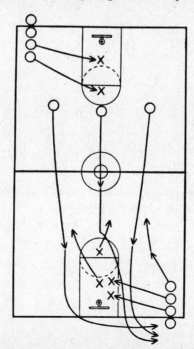

**Diagram 7**

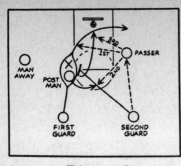

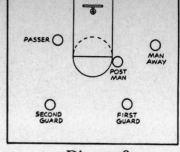

Diagram 8                    Diagram 9

to stop the first three. Two defensive players will be waiting for them at the other end of the floor.

This is an excellent drill for conditioning since there is quite a bit of movement involved.

### OFFENSIVE SET

As stated, our offense is the continuous type. Each player is named instead of numbered—first guard, second guard, passer, man away, and post man. Our offense starts with the second guard passing to the passer (Diagram 8). As the ball is being passed, the first guard cuts off the post man, looking for the pass. The second guard moves and screens for the post man, who moves toward the head of the circle for the shot. The second guard pivots and rolls toward the basket after the switch, looking for the ball. This gives us an opportunity for four shots or options.

### NEW SETUP

After we have run the shuffle, our new setup will be as follows: The man away has moved up as the new post man. The first guard has moved through and out as the man away. The second guard has rolled and moved around as the new passer. The post man stopped and moved out as the second guard on the left. The passer moved out as the first guard on the right side (Diagram 9).

Our style of offense gives each boy on the team the opportunity to play every position and handle the ball, plus providing everyone with the chance for the shot. Thus, our drill program is designed accordingly—we want teamwork and we get it.

# 3

# SITUATION DRILLS

## by Tom Brosnihan

*Head Basketball Coach*
*Creighton (Omaha, Nebraska) Preparatory School*

In nine years as head basketball coach at Creighton Preparatory (Omaha, Nebraska) School, Tom Brosnihan has compiled an overall record of 154 wins against 45 losses. His squads have taken their share of league, district, and state titles in that time.

At Creighton Prep, we believe that games are won on the practice floor. Our practices are very competitive, and we try to make every minute of practice similar to game-like conditions. The immediate result is that our boys respond to them.

### Breakdown of Defense and Offense

Our purpose is to break down our team pattern (both offensive and defensive) into one-on-one, two-on-two, or three-on-three situations. The nucleus of our practice schedule is here. Before the breakdown occurs, our players are conditioned and taught the proper position, stance, and footwork. Pete Newell's "hands-up drills" prepare our players the best.

### Situation Drills

The following series of diagrams illustrate how we break down our defenses into situations. Also, they give the offensive man a way out by throwing the ball to the feeder; thus, he can start over if he feels he cannot beat his man.

200

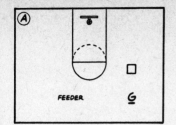

Diagram 1a

Diagram 1b

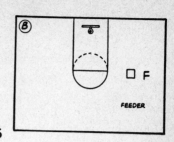

**ONE-ON-ONE SITUATIONS**

*Diagram 1a:* G has the ball; he drives and passes off to the feeder, etc., in order to beat his man. We work all the offensive and defensive skills on each player.

*Diagram 1b:* Forward or post. Here we use the forward with a feeder, or we can defense the post.

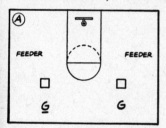

Diagram 2a

Diagram 2b

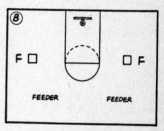

**TWO-ON-TWO SITUATIONS**

*Diagram 2a:* Front line (guard to guard). Two guards working together on all situations; switches; single and double cuts; screens.

*Diagram 2b:* Back line (forward to forward). Two forwards working together on all situations; cuts.

*Diagram 3a:* Sideline (guard to forward). They work on all situations.

*Diagram 3b:* Situations which might be seen: (a) inside screen; (b) slide screen; (c) blind pick.

*Diagram 4a:* We are defensing the post with double cutters or a single rub-out. We are working with the guard, forward, and post man.

*Diagram 4b:* Same as 4a, except we are using the guards and post man.

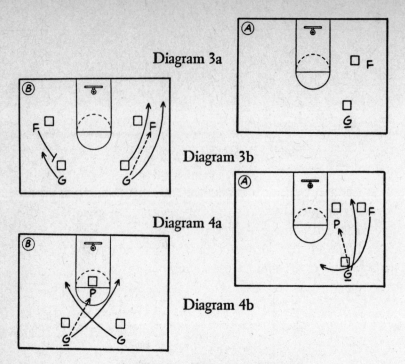

Diagram 3a

Diagram 3b

Diagram 4a

Diagram 4b

## THREE-ON-THREE SITUATIONS

*Diagram 5a:* We are noticing that more teams are concentrating a larger portion of their offense on weakside motion. So in this breakdown, we use the strong-side forward and guard with the weakside forward.

*Diagram 5b:* One of our best drills is our rotation drill in which we practice sliding through. We either do it with three men versus three men or four men versus four men.

Diagram 5a                    Diagram 5b

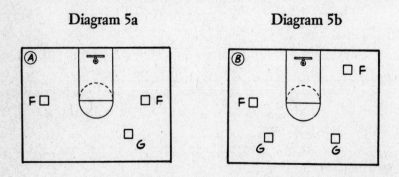

# 4

# SIX-STATION
# DRILL CIRCUIT

## by Dennis Walling

*Head Basketball Coach*
*West Texas (Canyon, Texas) State University*

Dennis Walling has been coaching college basketball since 1959 and has compiled an impressive 243–112 record during that time. At Decatur (Texas) Baptist College, he posted a 138–55 mark; at Dallas (Texas) Baptist College, he posted a 46–18 mark; at his present post, West Texas State University, he posted a 59–39 mark. The article that appears here is based on his coaching at Decatur Baptist College.

**O**ur six-station basketball drill circuit is an important aspect of our practice sessions at Decatur Baptist College. It keeps from 12 to 15 boys active and productive at the same time—and is excellent for both conditioning and working on fundamentals. We use it for about 20 minutes each day during preseason work.

Place two or more men at each station, depending on your squad, and have them work on specific drills for a total of three minutes each. When the whistle blows, they rotate to their right to begin the next drill. Here are the drills we work at each station (Diagram 1).

### STATION 1—ISOMETRICS

We use these exercises—the full extension, both flat-footed and the toe rise; the shoulder exercise, both flat-footed and the toe rise; and the pull exercise from the hips with the toe exercise.

**Diagram 1**

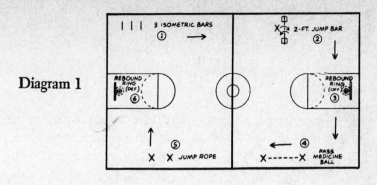

### STATION 2—JUMP BAR

Set up a high-jump bar about 2 feet off the floor by placing each end in the seat portion of folding chairs. The player faces the bar and jumps flat-footed over and back across the bar in a continuous movement—jumping over forward, and then back over backwards as fast as possible for three minutes.

### STATION 3—REBOUND RINGS (OFFENSE)

Here we work at improving our tip-ins. Two players, each side of the basket, rebound and try to tap the ball back in as high and quickly as possible.

### STATION 4—MEDICINE BALL

The medicine ball is passed between two players about 12 feet apart. The chest pass and the high pass are the ones we practice here.

### STATION 5—JUMP ROPE

We believe that jumping rope is a "must" for all basketball players; it's a good basic conditioner.

### STATION 6—REBOUND RINGS (DEFENSE)

Put a player on each side of the basket, with a rebound ring covering the goal. Pitch the ball up on the rim and let either player go up as high and strong as possible to rebound the ball with both hands. Have the player come down protecting the ball, pivoting, and getting it out to the outlet player (coach or manager) .

# 5

# GAME-CONDITION DRILLS

**by Ergie R. Smith, Jr.**

*Former Head Basketball Coach*
*Gary (West Virginia) High School*

In four years as head basketball coach, Ergie Smith
has led his Gary High School team to two sectional
championships, one regional championship, and two
state championships. At present he is teaching at
Gary, but plans to return to coaching in the near
future.

In basketball, as in most sports, the team that makes the least mistakes usually wins. To minimize making mistakes under game conditions, we emphasize drills to develop the basic fundamentals of the game, and add something to them to make them as much like game play as possible. Repetition without challenge becomes monotonous.

Here are a few of our drills, and the basketball fundamental each individual drill tries to perfect.

## CLUB DRILL

This drill is used to develop dribbling skill; we find it most helpful in keeping the dribbler's eyes "out of the floor."

We put one offensive player in each corner of the gym; the boys on the same side work with each other (Diagram 1). The dribbler reacts to his partner's moves. For example, the dribbler starts out being harassed by a de-

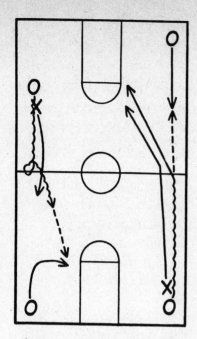

Diagram 1

Diagram 2

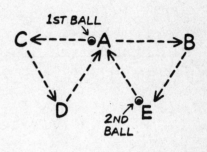

fensive player (X). The offensive partner without the ball may: (1) stay on the spot; (2) move out toward the dribbler; or (3) cut for the basket. The dribbler reacts as follows: If (1) occurs, he cuts for the basket; if (2) occurs, he passes to his partner and cuts; if (3) occurs, he passes to his partner under the basket. Note from the diagram:

- On the *right*, offensive player O dribbles to make a complete pivot pass-off to the player breaking under the basket.

- On the *left*, offensive player O dribbles and passes off to the player breaking up, and cuts for the basket.

### PASS REACTION DRILL

We use this drill to improve the reaction of our players to passes and teach them how to employ different types of passes accurately.

Two balls are used with five men working together (Diagram 2); three men are in one line, and two in another parallel line. The ball is given to the middle man in the three-man line. He may pass to either man beside him; these men may pass to either man in the opposite line. The second ball is given to either man in the two-man line, who may pass to the middle man in the three-man line in a continuous rotation.

This drill may be executed with more men, and it is suggested that the boys shift positions every two minutes.

It works this way: As soon as A passes the first ball to C, E passes the second ball to A. In the meantime, C is passing the first ball to D, and A is passing the second ball to B. D passes the first ball to A, B passes the second ball to E, and the drill repeats itself without lost motion.

### BOUNCE-PASS DRILL

We use this drill to improve bounce-pass techniques. We use three men—an offensive and defensive man on one side of the court, and another offensive man on the other (Diagram 3). We stress this rule: In making a bounce pass to a moving target past a defensive man, you must bounce the ball at the defensive man's feet at an angle that will get past his feet and come up so your teammate can catch it. It is a fact that you cannot run at full speed and react as low as your feet; this is why the pass is made at the feet of the defender.

To help improve defensive skills, we instruct the defensive man not to move until the offensive man does; he must keep his eye on the offensive player without the ball.

### LOOP-PASS DRILL

For those occasions when a loop pass is called for, we use this drill to avoid the common dangers: the pass to the free man is too straight, is overshot, or is knocked down by a defender.

Three men work together; a receiver, a passer, and a defender (Diagram 4). We have all players moving toward

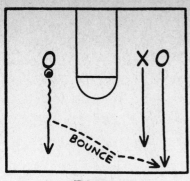

**Diagram 3**

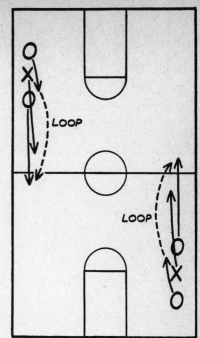

**Diagram 4**

the basket, with the defender keying off the receiver so he won't take advantage and move out too quickly. We coach the receivers to catch the ball before it hits the ground if possible, but we show them that if the ball has the proper loop, it can be caught even if it hits the floor.

We occasionally use smaller balls to improve passing and receiving.

### REBOUNDING DRILLS

These drills are used to coach the six fundamentals in good rebounding:

a. Maintain a wide base in jumping.
b. Position to permit the player to jump slightly forward as well as upward.
c. Jump to reach ball at apex of jump.
d. Keep spread in the air.
e. Use two hands (if possible) to control ball.
f. Snatch ball from air, bringing it to a protective position similar to the first position of the two-hand chest pass.

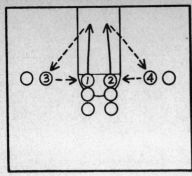

**Diagram 5**

I'm sure that many coaches will note that this is not a conventional drill, because we place the boys 12 to 15 feet from the basket, as the diagram will show. We do this because we feel the boys will move into the basket for the ball and jump up and out for it. We have found that the conventional drills have the boys jumping upward only and this way they'll never out-rebound a better jumper or taller man.

Two lines of players, (1) and (2), are facing the backboard with a ball for each line (Diagram 5). Two additional lines of players, (3) and (4), are at the free-throw line to receive an outlet pass. A rebound ring is in the basket. The lines alternate with each player in lines (1) and (2) shooting the ball, moving in for the rebound, and shooting an outlet pass. The player getting the outlet pass returns it to the next player in lines (1) and (2). Players rotate from the rebounding line to the outlet line to the opposite rebounding line.

### Variation 1

This covers the same fundamentals, plus body control in the air. Players line up and alternate as in the basic drill. They leave the floor facing the base line, rebound the ball, twist the body in the air, and land facing the sideline.

### Variation 2

This teaches the defensive part of the blockout. The first players in the line assume a defensive stance opposite the next players. On the shot, they screen and block out while the offensive player tries to rebound and make an outlet pass or tip in. Offensive and defensive players interchange, and no fouling should be allowed.

No drill is a magic wand for victory; we think, however, that these drills will help you along the road.

# 6

# THREE TAP-IN DRILLS

## by James Fulghum

*Head Basketball Coach*
*Green Central (Snow Hill, North Carolina) High School*

James Fulghum has been coaching high school basketball since 1962. In two years as head basketball coach at North Edgecomb (Tarboro, North Carolina) High School, he posted a fantastic 51–5 mark which included a state championship. At present, he is head basketball coach at Green Central High School and has an overall record of 141–55.

Not enough is said or done about the tap-in. It is a quick-scoring opportunity too often missed. Many times a player can get boxed out under the board and still get one hand on the ball. We pick up a lot of baskets on tap-ins; we have scored when it is impossible to come down with a rebound.

The tap-in requires good wrist action and finger control. We practice it at least twice a week. Here are three of our favorite drills:

1. The boys form two lines (Diagram 1). X-1 and X-2 tap the ball off the board two times, into the basket the third time, and go to the end of the line.
2. X-2 throws the ball against the board and X-1 taps it in. After five taps, X-1 and X-2 interchange (Diagram 2). Each boy will tap 15 times before the drill is over.
3. The coach is the shooter. On the shot, X-1 and X-3 keep trying for a tap-in basket until X-2 comes down with the rebound (Diagram 3).

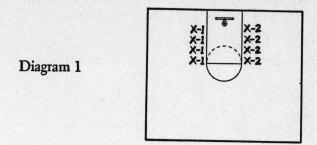

Diagram 1

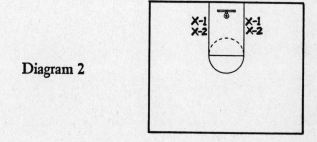

Diagram 2

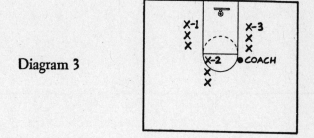

Diagram 3

# 7

## TEN-IN-ONE DRILL

**by Sonny Clements**

*Head Basketball Coach*
*Columbus (Georgia) College*

Columbus College competed in intercollegiate athletics for the first time in 1959–60, the second year of the school's operation. From a 2–15 record that year, Coach Frank "Sonny" Clements has taken his basketball team to a 158–93 overall record and three second-place finishes in the tough Georgia JCAA Conference.

I call this drill my ten-in-one drill because it teaches *at least* ten basketball fundamentals from a single practice formation. Working on the fundamentals from the same formation saves time and gets the job done.

In each of the diagrams below, I will indicate the basketball fundamental being worked in *italic* type. Count them up, if you wish. No fundamental is repeated in italics.

*Diagram 1:* Middle man *dribbles* hard and fast to free-throw line, *fakes* pass to opposite side, then *passes* to side man. Side man *receives* fast pass and *shoots lay-up*. Middle man takes ball out of basket, steps out-of-bounds, and makes *baseball pass* to shooter, who has continued on around to receive the outlet pass. He receives pass, turns, makes a couple of dribbles, and executes *chest pass* to next middle man. Middle man goes to right line and side man goes to middle.

If shot is missed, middle man *rebounds* and makes *outlet pass* to shooter.

217

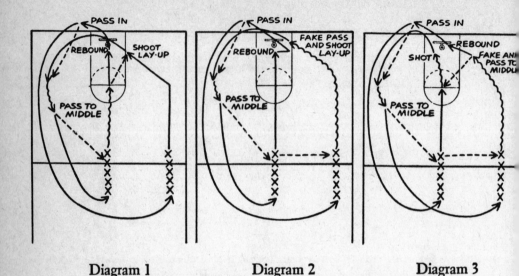

**Diagram 1**            **Diagram 2**            **Diagram 3**

*Diagram* 2: Middle man passes to side man and goes deep to act as dummy defense. Side man dribbles, fakes pass to imaginary player, and shoots driving *crip shot*. Defense can harass shooter to simulate game conditions. Middle man rebounds and makes baseball outlet pass to side man, who has continued around. Drill finishes as in Diagram 1.

*Diagram* 3: Middle man passes to side man, who dribbles hard down the side and passes to middle man on free-throw line, who dribbles in and shoots crip shot. Side man rebounds, steps out-of-bounds, and throws baseball pass to middle man who has continued around. Middle man takes shot, turns, dribbles, and makes chest pass to next middle man.

This repeats fundamentals, but from different floor positions.

*Diagram 4*: Middle man dribbles a couple of times and passes to side man, who dribbles down side, fakes, and passes to middle man at free-throw line for *jump shot*. Side man rebounds and makes outlet pass to middle man, who has gone around. Drill completes as others.

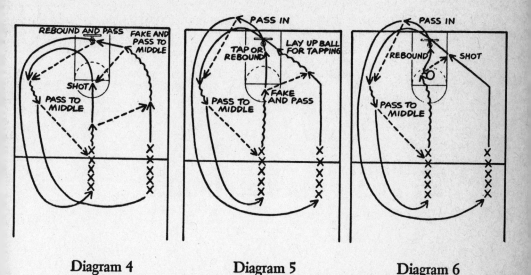

**Diagram 4**                    **Diagram 5**                    **Diagram 6**

*Diagram 5:* Middle man dribbles to free-throw line, fakes to opposite side, and passes to side man. Side man dribbles hard and shoots ball up on goal. Middle man follows ball and *tips* it into basket, then takes ball out-of-bounds and makes outlet pass to side man, who has gone around. Drill completes as others.

By using a goal cover, the drill becomes one for *defensive* rebounding.

*Diagram 6:* Place defensive man (O) in three-second lane. Middle man dribbles down and forces defensive man to play him. When defensive man commits himself, middle man passes to side man, who drives in for shot in a typical *two-on-one* situation. Defensive man rebounds the shot and makes outlet pass to side man, who has continued around. Side man goes to middle, middle man stays to play defense, and defensive man goes to sideline.

# 8

# SCRAMBLE:
# A GAME-SITUATION DRILL

**by Gary R. Apsey**

*Assistant Basketball Coach*
*Arthur Hill (Saginaw, Michigan) High School*

Gary Apsey graduated from Central Michigan University in 1963 with a B.S. degree in Physical Education. He coached freshman football and basketball at Schafer (Southgate, Michigan) High School for two years and then moved to St. Charles (Michigan) High School in 1965. At present, he is assistant basketball coach at Arthur Hill High School. His overall record to date is 78–44.

**S**cramble is a game-situation drill that is ideal for basketball. It involves the many skills used in the game and it helps to promote hustle, desire, and enthusiasm.

The game is played with five players at the free-throw area, as shown in Diagram 1. Two players are on defense and assume the defensive position on the free-throw lane nearest the end line. Two players on offense take the adjacent position on the free-throw lane. The fifth player (third offensive player) is at the free-throw line.

The player at the free-throw line shoots a maximum of five free throws in succession. For every free throw made, his team receives one point. If he misses his free throw, the other four players try to get the rebound and score a field goal.

The defensive team supplies a free-throw shooter if they score a field goal; the offensive team has the free-throw shooter if they score the field goal off the rebound.

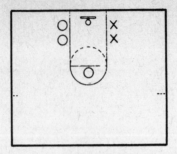

**Diagram 1**

The offensive and defensive players change positions on the lane according to the situation. Field goals count 2 points, free throws 1 point, and the cumulative score can be any number desired.

Frequent fouling and violations should be eliminated by the players themselves. Boundaries should confine play to the one basket area. There isn't any out-of-bounds in this game.

Rebounding, free-throw shooting, defense, and offense are some of the many skills employed in this drill. Modifications can be made to stress offense or defense and encourage rebounding, hustle, desire, and enthusiasm.

# 9

# DRILLS TO PERFECT FUNDAMENTALS

## by Don Morris

*Head Basketball Coach*
*East Hardin (Glendale, Kentucky) High School*

Don Morris came to Breckinridge County (Hardins-
burg, Kentucky) High School in 1960 as junior varsity
coach, and ended the season with a 15–4 record. He
became head coach the following year. His seven-
year record there was 154–52 and included three
district titles, two regional, two state runner-up, and
one state title. At present, he is head basketball
coach at East Hardin; his overall record to date is
214–81. Parker Publishing Company recently put out
his book, *Kentucky High School Basketball*

**R**egardless of how much basketball knowledge a team possesses, it will not be successful—especially under pressure—unless all players are fundamentally sound. It makes no difference if the entire squad knows a dozen unique plays that will definitely produce; if they can't dribble, pass, shoot, and run—how can the play be completed? The basics of the game make the play work.

The fundamentals of basketball can't be stressed too often. This phase of the game is probably taken for granted more than any other—especially after the season is under way. Instead, they should play an important part in practice sessions throughout the season, even the week before tournaments.

Here are some drills we use with our squad to perfect basketball fundamentals; they have done the job for us.

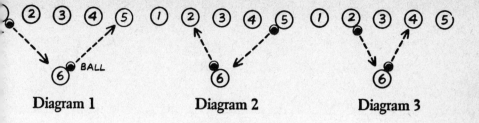

Diagram 1          Diagram 2          Diagram 3

## PASSING

### Peripheral Vision

With the peripheral vision drill, the team is divided into groups—six boys to a group (Diagram 1). Five boys stand in a straight line with one boy out front; two balls are used. One ball starts at the end of the line and the other with the man out front. At the sound of the whistle, the ball is passed from 1 to 6 and simultaneously from 6 to 5 (Diagram 1). Immediately upon receiving the pass from 1, 6 passes the ball to 2 and simultaneously 5 passes to 6 (Diagram 2). Player 6 then passes to 4 and receives the ball from 2 (Diagram 3). Passes are made to all men and then reversed until the ball is in the original position or until a specified number of minutes elapse. If a ball is dropped or there is a bad pass, the drill is started over.

We place emphasis on sharp, quick, accurate passes chest high. The drill improves peripheral vision, accurate passing, and helps develop teamwork.

### Passing Through

The passing-through drill is performed with two men facing each other, and a third man in the middle. The middle man must advance forward to the man with the ball (who must wait until the middle man is closely guarding him) and force him to make a reverse pivot to protect the ball, make various fakes, and the pass necessary to complete the play. The defensive man's objective is to touch the ball, deflect it, or cause a dropped ball or bad pass. In this case, a bad pass is one whereby the receiver has to take more than one step to catch the ball.

If any of the violations occur, the middle man is replaced by the violator. The drill helps improve a boy's ability to make good fakes and a variety of passes under pressure.

## DRIBBLING

Here are three drills that have been most effective in improving our dribbling. In each, we stress staying low, keeping the head up and the eyes off the ball, and changing hands with the dribble.

### Drill 1

Place a leader out front, and the remainder of the boys facing the leader in parallel straight lines with four or five boys to a line. The drill begins with all the boys kneeling on one knee, dribbling the ball to the side with head up watching the leader. When "position" is called, the boys, still dribbling the ball, take a crouch position. When the whistle is blown, the boys move in the same direction as the leader. As the leader moves left, right, forward, backward, and changes hands with the dribble, they do as he does. It is essential that the boys keep their eyes on the leader rather than watch the ball.

### Drill 2

Position six or seven boys, 3 to 4 feet apart, in a straight line up the middle of the court. The other players, each with a basketball, start at the end of the line and dribble in a zigzag pattern around each man. After reaching the end of the line, the dribbler turns and dribbles as fast as possible straight up the floor to the original position. He continues this pattern until the whistle is blown.

Emphasize the necessity to dribble with as much speed as possible and still maintain ball control. Also stress dribbling to the outside of each player, thus keeping the ball to the farthest point from the defensive man and making it necessary to change hands while dribbling.

### Drill 3

Diagram 4 illustrates this dribbling drill. Start in the corner at the end of the floor as shown, and continue as follows: dribble across the base line up the side of the court to opposite the key hole—turn and dribble across the floor to the key hole around the head of the circle to the opposite key hole and across the floor to the other side—go up the sideline to the midcourt stripe, make a sharp turn, and dribble across the floor—make a sharp turn at the opposite sideline and follow the out-of-bounds line until opposite the key hole —turn as at the beginning of the drill and continue until the leader is in the opposite corner on the other end of the floor

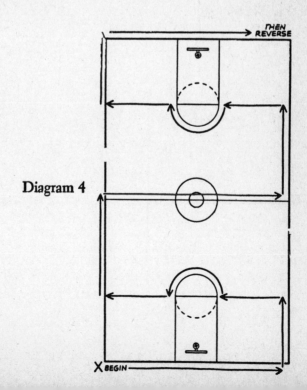

Diagram 4

than originally. Reverse direction and follow the same pattern until the last man in the original formation is in the corner where the drill began.

Emphasize making sharp cuts across the corners and around the circle and maintaining as great a speed as possible with good ball control.

### COMBINING FUNDAMENTALS

We use several drills which combine various fundamentals; here are some of them.

**Diagram 5**

Divide the boys into two straight lines—one line on each end of the court. Place a chair near the center circle on the midcourt line (Diagram 5). The first boy in group A dribbles the ball rapidly up the floor and makes a pass to the first man in group B, who advances forward and meets the

Diagram 5

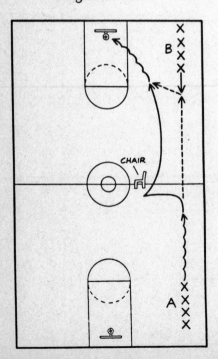

Diagram 6

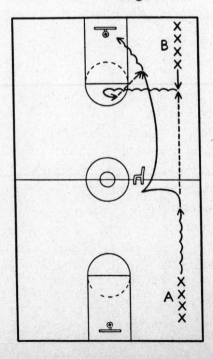

pass. After passing, A takes two or three more steps forward, fakes toward the inside of the chair, plants his foot, pushes off in the opposite direction, goes around the chair on the outside, cuts toward the goal, receives the pass from B—and shoots the lay-up. A then goes to the back of line B and B goes to the back of line A.

### Diagram 6

This drill is the same as that shown in Diagram 5 through A cutting for the basket—with the variation that B dribbles across the floor to the free-throw line and reverses his pivot while A is making his fake around the chair. From this new position, B then passes to A who is driving by for the shot (Diagram 6).

### Diagram 7

This is the same as the drill in Diagram 5 through A making his fake around the chair. A then cuts down beside B, gets a return pass, takes one or two dribbles, immediately does a reverse pivot, and hands off to B, who is cutting by for the pass and the jump shot or lay-up (Diagram 7).

Each variation helps to improve footwork, passing, and shooting.

### Diagram 8

Here's an excellent drill to improve ball-handling ability, dribbling, pivoting, changing of pace, changing of direction, and shooting of several kinds of shots. It's also a good conditioner. The drill uses 12 chairs placed as follows: three on the side, one on the side at the base line, one at the head of the circle, one at the free-throw line, and the other six in the same arrangement on the other end of the court (Diagram 8).

The players form a line on the end of the floor opposite the three chairs on the side (Part A). The first player

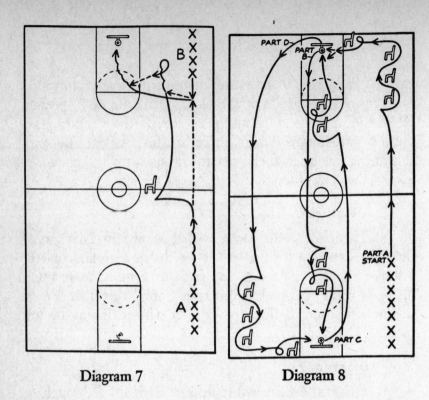

| Diagram 7 | Diagram 8 |

dribbles toward the three chairs, using a change of pace until he reaches the first chair. He then fakes to the inside, plants his foot, pushes off in the opposite direction, and goes around the outside of the chair. Immediately upon passing the first chair, it is necessary to change direction to the inside of the second chair and also change hands while dribbling. The dribbler then goes around the third chair in the same way and continues dribbling down the base line until he is cut off by the one chair.

He then does a reverse dribble, rolls around the chair at the base line, and shoots any of the following shots: fall-away jump shot, regular jump shot after cutting across the lane, regular lay-up after rolling around the chair, or back-over-the-head lay-up while going all the way under the goal and shooting on the opposite side.

After taking the ball out of the net, he dribbles up the middle of the court (Part B) to the first chair at the head of the opposite circle, fakes, plants his foot at one side of the chair, pushes off and changes direction, goes around the chair, immediately encounters the second chair on the free-throw line, plants his foot, does a reverse dribble, rolls around the chair, and shoots the lay-up on either side of the goal, or the jump shot.

The player, after making the shot, drives the length of the court (Part C), makes the same moves around the chairs at the head of the circle and the free-throw line, and takes another shot. He then dribbles up the far side of the floor (Part D) using his change of pace until he reaches the first of the last three chairs, makes the same moves as he did with the first three chairs, and then encounters the last chair of the drill at the base line. After making the fourth shot of the drill, he takes his position at the back of the line—and the next player begins the drill.

# 10

## DRILL WITH A
## MULTIPLE PURPOSE

**by Jack Stanford**

*Head Basketball Coach*
*Baylor (Chattanooga, Tennessee) School for Boys*

Jack Stanford has been head basketball coach at Baylor School for Boys since 1960. His overall record there is 179–87, including four mid-South tournaments and championships.

Every basketball coach strives to obtain maximum effort from his players. We believe one method of achieving this is to have drills that are instructional and interesting— even fun in most instances. Also, since practice time is limited in most high schools, we use drills that develop more than one phase of the fundamentals and skills necessary to play sound basketball. The following drill is a case in point.

Our favorite drill is one that develops about ten different skills in a minimum amount of time. We call it the "killer" because it takes maximum energy to perform it properly. The full court is used for the drill.

Here's how we set up and run our killer drill.

## DRILL ALIGNMENT

We begin with the alignment shown in Diagram 1. Numbers 1, 2, and 3 break down

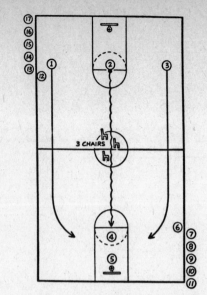

Diagram 1

the floor in a regular 3-on-2 fast-break pattern, with number 2 dribbling the ball through the chairs and on down the middle of the floor toward his goal. The chairs are used not only to make the dribbler be alert for a defensive man at half-court and to practice dribbling skills, but to help with the proper timing of the drill.

As the drill progresses, the middle man has a tendency to get too far ahead of his wing men on the fast-break pattern. All three players should arrive at their designated spots at about the same time. Proper timing will do it.

## THE DRIBBLER

The dribbler is instructed to move as close to the free-throw line as the defense will permit. He must keep his eyes on the two defensive men and determine his next move from their defensive actions. Making him watch the defensive men promotes better dribbling techniques and peripheral vision—as he must see the progress of his wing men out of the corner of his eye.

If the front defensive man stops the dribbler's progress and then sags back to defend on one of the wing men, the middle man is coached to take the good percentage shot im-

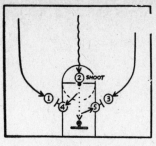

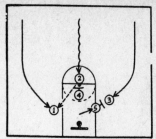

Diagram 2                              Diagram 3

mediately from around the free-throw line (Diagram 2). If
the front man plays him, he is coached to look through to the
second defender and pass to the wing away from this defender
(Diagram 3).

Our middle man is instructed to remain at the free-
throw line throughout the action—except to go for a rebound
that bounces back at him.

### THE WING MEN

The wing men break down the floor at a wide angle.
Some coaches prefer a straighter more direct angle—but we
prefer the wide angle for two reasons: it's easier for the
middle men to see the wing man and pass to him; it's more
difficult to defense this wide approach with only one or two
defenders. The wing men must be careful not to break beyond the backboard. If they do not receive the pass by the
time they reach the three-second lane, they stop and set up a
triangle with the middle man (Diagram 4).

The wing men are coached not to cross the three-
second lane since it causes too much congestion under the
goal. The ball is passed around the triangle until a good shot
is taken. Passes across the lane from one wing to the other are
discouraged unless it's certain that the pass will get through.

Since this is a difficult pass and can be defended
against in most cases, our middle man is required to remain
at the free-throw line where a quick pass back to him will find
him open a majority of the time.

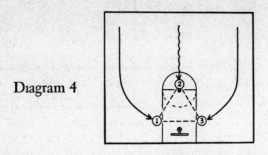

Diagram 4

## THE DEFENSIVE MEN

The two defensive men line up in a tandem and play regular 3-on-2 defense until the ball is either rebounded by the defense or a goal is made by the offense. In either case, the ball is thrown to number 6 who is breaking toward the middle to receive the pass. He must dribble through the chairs for proper timing (Diagram 5). Numbers 4 and 5 fill the wing lanes.

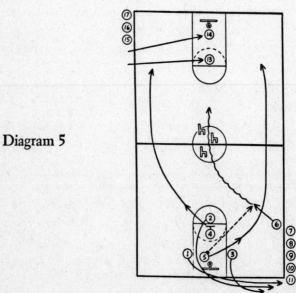

Diagram 5

We do not fill a particular lane a certain way in our regular game offense. Our defense is primarily man-for-man, so we're never sure of what position our players will be in when we rebound the ball. They are simply told to fill the lane nearest them—and if someone is already there, find another one.

Numbers 1, 2, and 3 move off the floor and get at the end of the line—and numbers 13 and 14 move onto the floor to defend against 4, 5, and 6.

## Fundamentals and Skills

Five to eight minutes of this drill daily will improve your team because it develops numerous fundamentals and skills: dribbling and ball handling; passing; peripheral vision; filling the lanes; 3-on-2 offense and defense shooting; offensive rebounding; blocking out and defensive rebounding; speed and hustle—and of course, it serves as an excellent conditioner.

# 11

# REBOUND AND FREE-THROW DRILL

**by Clarence Moore, Ph.D.**

*Chairman,*
*Department of Health and Physical Education*
*Bloomsburg (Pa.) State College*

Dr. Clarence Moore is Chairman of the Department of Health and Physical Education at Bloomsburg (Pa.) State College. He held a similar position at the University of Alabama and coached basketball in Michigan High Schools. At present he is involved in teacher training at Bloomsburg.

**H**ere's a drill that will enliven that mid- or late-season practice and at the same time accomplish the following:

- promote aggressive rebounding;
- improve free-throw shooting;
- provide practice on set offenses and defenses in a controlled situation;
- provide practice on offense and defense in out-of-bounds situations;
- provide a new, highly motivated, and competitive game situation, with emphasis on offensive play, defensive play, and foul shooting.

### PROCEDURE

Select ten players to begin the contest —designating five as offensive and five as defensive. The group designated as the offense remains on the attack as long as they score or rebound the ball. The game is played half-court and under one goal. All offensive baskets

239

count 2 points, and possession is retained by the offense after each score. After every field goal, the offensive team puts the ball in play from the base line under the basket—thus facilitating practice on out-of-bounds play situations.

When the offense fails to score and loses the rebound, or commits a violation—the defense becomes the offense in a free-throw situation. Each player of the defensive team then moves in turn to the line and shoots two free throws—provided each shot is made or his team recovers the missed attempt.

In rebounding the ball, however, the free-throw team must successfully move the ball beyond the free-throw line again before they can claim control of the ball and resume foul shooting. No player may shoot more than two shots in succession and he must shoot these shots in turn—with relationship to his teammates. Thus, if a player misses his first free throw and his team does not rebound the missed attempt, he cannot return to the line for his second shot until his team again recovers possession of the ball.

A game consists of 10 points by either team—with the teams then changing roles (the free-throw team becomes the offense and vice versa). Jump-ball situations are handled by alternately awarding possession to each team.

With a little practice, you will probably find that the two teams approximate the same number of points—thus creating a tense competitive situation. The boys may become a little too aggressive both on the boards and defensively—but this can be remedied by officiating as needed.

# 12

# JUMPING AND REBOUNDING DRILL

**by Gene Stewart**

*Athletic Director*
*Iowa School (Council Bluffs, Iowa) for the Deaf*

Before coming to the Iowa School for the Deaf, Gene Stewart coached basketball at Treynor (Iowa) High School, where he compiled an overall mark of 135–87. At his present post, he is vocational guidance counselor as well as the athletic director. The following article is based on his work at Treynor High School.

Every coach knows the importance of co-ordination, timing, and general reflex action in the basketball player. It becomes even more important in coaching the deaf boy, because of the destruction of the inner ear. I have found the simple drill described below to be a tremendous time-saver in conditioning, jumping, and rebounding. In the early season, we spend 20 minutes a day on it; as the season progresses, we cut the time in half, but do not abandon it.

Prior to coming to the Iowa School for the Deaf, I coached high school basketball for nine years; the drill works well as a time-saver for boys with hearing.

Here is how it works (see Diagram 1): We line the boys up as shown. Using one ball, we start the first boy toward the basket. He dribbles, jumps, and puts the ball against the board; the others follow on the run, jumping, rebounding, and putting the ball back on the board for the next boy in line to do the same.

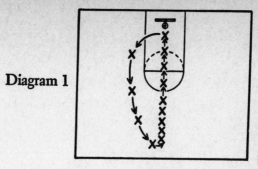

Diagram 1

We use ten or 12 boys on each board, and it is easy to keep the entire squad busy.

By putting the ball on the board, I mean catch, control, and place the ball on the board in the jumping motion. The ball is put on the board as if the boy were trying for a goal on the rebound.

Note these points:

- We space the boys in the line so they do not get a chance to stand around and wait for a rebound.
- The first boy in line is the only one who does any dribbling, and one aim of the drill is to see how long you can keep it going without the ball hitting the ground.
- If you demand perfection of all skills on this drill, you will find it to be a good conditioner, too.
- Keep boys with equal ability on each board; this speeds up the drill.
- Make sure the boys lay the ball back up on the board (do not bat or throw), the same as if they were following to score a basket

# 13

## SELECTED
## SPEED-UP DRILLS

**by Dario Soto**

*Head Basketball Coach*
*Medicine Bow (Wyoming) High School*

Dario Soto graduated from the University of Wyoming in 1963, and coached three years at Fort Laramie (Wyoming) High School before moving to Medicine Bow (Wyoming) High School as head basketball coach in 1966. In 1967, his team had an 18–4 record and was fourth in the state tournament. In the following year, Coach Soto's team won the state championship. His record at Medicine Bow is 69–37.

**M**edicine Bow High School is in Class C or the smallest category in the Wyoming sports scale, because it has fewer than 50 students. Obviously a coach in such a school does not have a large group nor a choice one at his command, and must try to be resourceful to fill out a varsity squad.

Although basketball attracts most of the school's male population, I have had to work with as few as eight boys, and 20 has been the high.

### Rating Candidates

In the group that turns out for basketball, we find some who know the fundamentals, a few more who are acquainted with the game but do not have a working knowledge, and the rest who come out because others do.

I see a few boys who are well coordinated, others who are somewhat coordinated, and those who have trouble standing up.

In a larger school with far more prospective players, the weaker candidates would be rooted out ruthlessly, but we have got to make do.

### Division by Skill

In order to incorporate as many candidates as possible, we have devised a graduated pattern of training based on skill, or the lack of it. There are three divisions.

In the No. 1 talent group are the few boys with experience who can regain their peak of the past season with just a little work.

In the middle group are those who need polishing but do have a grasp of the basics. The third group is green and needs a crash program.

Ultimately, in this hurry-up system, we hope to secure enough competent players for a junior varsity as well as a first-string team.

### Allotting Practice

Generally the first two weeks of practice are for drills and conditioning, and the final two for setting up offense and defense.

However, the weakest third of the squad may still be heavily engaged in drills to perfect techniques into the third week, while the strongest third of the squad may have begun the study of strategy and tactics in the first week.

In the first two weeks, I divide my time into four parts. I spend one-fourth with each of the three skill divisions, and the remaining fourth with all candidates in a group, to sum up my impressions of the day and foster the idea of one team and one spirit, despite our arbitrary division.

### Drill Routine

In our hurry-up scheme with the least proficient boys, we emphasize nine drills which stress fundamentals: dribbling (3), passing (2), and shooting (4).

These drills were selected after the most exhaustive study of coaching systems, clinics, magazine articles, books, and word of mouth that we could undertake.

In my opinion the nine drills will cover all fundamental points of basketball, in a small package.

### Drill Procedure

To encourage participation and to make sure a drill is taken for more than a time-filler, we explain each one to the team, stating the purpose and its importance to the team.

Furthermore, each drill is walked out first so that the reason for each move may be clarified, and only then is the tempo increased.

In this way a boy can analyze a drill for himself, with out pressure, to form his own opinion on its proper execution and its value.

### DRIBBLING DRILLS

### Stop and Go

The coach will act as traffic director, using hand signals indicating where the boy must dribble. The dribbler obviously must watch the coach to get the signal, and in doing this he cannot look at the ball, therefore acquiring needed finesse

### One-on-One

This is a play started from midcourt to teach the dribbler to activate a decision at full speed. That is, he is to drive hard for the basket to score a lay-up, as if he saw such an opportunity in competition. He is opposed in this drill by a limited defense.

An added benefit of this simple drill is the help it affords us in our man-on-man defense.

### Free Dribble

This drill is a great favorite of the players because

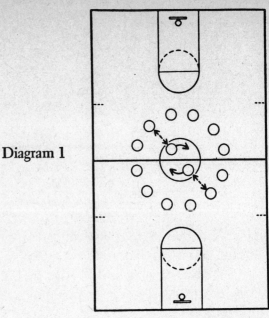

Diagram 1

there is competition and a chance to express individuality and personal skills.

Using the full court, four or five dribblers will start on whistle for the far basket. Each may dribble in any direction he desires and may slap at another's ball, so long as he continues dribbling.

On a second whistle, the dribblers drive for a lay-up, then rebound their own ball, and dribble quickly to the starting end of the court where another man begins the drill.

## PASSING DRILLS

### Two-Man Circle (Diagram 1)

Two men are placed in the middle of a circle of their teammates. They pass the ball to those in the circle, who move around in a clockwise or counterclockwise motion.

The first time around a chest pass is employed. Then a bounce pass is called for on the second go-round. A baseball pass is used on the third circle.

When a boy in the circle has completed the above drill, he exchanges places with one of the boys in the middle.

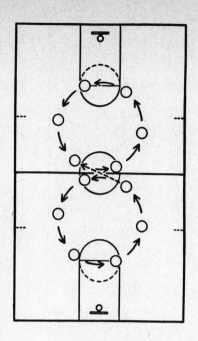

**Diagram 2**

## Bounce and Chest (Diagram 2)

The running bounce and chest drill is worked with two circles moving counterclockwise. On the rim of the circles a boy in one passes to a boy in the other, and this process continues.

After about 100, or even 150 good chest passes, the circles change to a bounce pass. Then the circles are run in reverse, and go through the drill again.

## SHOOTING DRILLS

Our shooting drills feature passing and driving towards the basket. We use a lot of give-and-go. All our shooting drills will work from either side of the court.

### Feed, Follow, and Pass (Diagram 3)

There is a file of players behind the foul line and another beyond the circle on the left court. The former are A players, the latter B players.

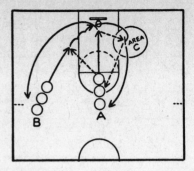

Diagram 3

Action opens with B cutting for the basket; A passes to him as he reaches the lane. After shooting, B crosses the lane. Meanwhile A has rushed in for the rebound, and passes to B in Area C. B passes to the next man in the A file.

The original player A moves to the rear of the B file, and the original B player to the end of the A file; this process continues throughout the drill.

### Jumper Give-and-Go (Diagram 4)

File A and file B line up at opposite sides of the court between the midcourt area and the head of the key. The ball may begin on either side.

### Diagram 4

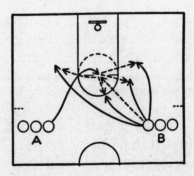

If a player in file B has the ball, then A cuts to the front of the free-throw line where he receives a pass from B. Then B will cut to any forward area he desires to receive a pass from A and jump shoot.

Both players will follow the shot for the rebound; then B will join the A line and vice versa.

### Open Shooting

The boys may shoot a jumper or a set shot in an area from 10 to 15 feet out.

### Free-Shot Routine

Each boy will throw 25 foul shots daily and keep a score. At the end of the first and second weeks, the coaches will consult the score and decide whether the boy needs more work or whether he is to advance.

# 14

## SKILL DRILLS

### by Bill Frohliger

*Head Basketball Coach*
*Bloomington (Indiana) High School*

In his 15 years of coaching basketball, Bill Frohliger spent eight years at Cathedral High School in Indianapolis. In spite of having had several losing seasons before he began to coach there, Cathedral High under his leadership went on to be ranked in the state for five years. In seven years as head basketball coach at Bloomington (Indiana) High School, Coach Frohliger has guided his squads to five sectional titles and three regionals. His overall mark is 206–141.

At Bloomington High School, we believe in using anything that can help improve our basketball program. Having already taken practice drills from baseball, ballet, and other activities, we adapted the "Crash Program"—a series of drills used by our football team—to basketball practice. We are convinced that our teams have greatly benefitted from its use.

The Crash Program is designed to improve many different skills, as well as develop better conditioning, reflexes, agility, and speed.

Here's how it works.

### Organization

We create four stations, each with a specific area of concentration: Station I–defense; Station II–shooting; Station III–offense movement; Station IV–rebounding. Each station may consist of one or many drills, depending on what is to be stressed at that particular time.

Early in the season—during tryouts—we divide the players into four groups and conduct the Crash Program on a daily basis. Each group is assigned to a station and remains there for eight minutes. As I have only one assistant coach, we operate one station each, while a manager supervises the other two and keeps track of the time as well. At a signal, each group moves on to the next station, continuing until everyone has been through all the stations.

As the season progresses, we reduce the number of times a week the program is held to three and then two, and finally possibly once a week. As the groups get smaller, we cut down the size of each group, using eight as a minimum number. Further, the time spent at each station may be reduced to as little as four minutes.

Once the team is selected, it is divided into two groups; whereupon, I take over responsibility for Stations III and IV, and my assistant assumes responsibility for Stations I and II.

The schedule of a single day's practice—shown in Chart I—will facilitate the understanding of how each of the four stations of the Crash Program is fitted into the overall practice session.

### STATION I

In this section of the program, we stress the defensive footwork drills.

#### Dummy en Masse Drills

As illustrated in Diagram 1, the movement of the players is directed by the coach.

#### Dummy 1-on-1 Drill

Here, the players are paired off and divided into two groups (Diagram 2). Each player guards his partner, then

## Early Season Practice Schedule

Before 4:00 P.M. —— Free shoot

4:00 - 4:10 P.M. —— Exercise

4:10 - 4:20 P.M. —— Warm-up drills (same as pregame)

4:20 - 4:52 P.M. —— CRASH PROGRAM

### STATION I
#### Defensive Footwork Drills

1. Dummy en masse drill ........................ 3 min.
2. Dummy 1-on-1 drill ......................... 3 min.
3. Defensive killer drill ...................... 1 min.
4. Reaction drill ................................. 1 min.

### STATION II
#### Shooting Drills

1. Half-court shooting drill on move .... 4 min.
2. Garbage drill ................................. 4 min.

### STATION III
#### Passing and Dribbling Drills

1. Four-corner passing drill ................. 4 min.
2. Dribble obstacle course .................. 4 min.

### STATION IV
#### Rebound Drills

1. 1-on-1 semi-circle drill ................... 6 min.
2. Reaction drill ............ .................. 2 min.

4:52 - 4:55 P.M. —— Break (water)

4:55 - 5:15 P.M. —— Guards routine: Mr. McMillan
Forward and Centers: Mr. Frohliger

5:15 - 5:30 P.M. —— Fast-break drill

5:30 - 5:40 P.M. —— Hamburger drill

5:40 - 5:45 P.M. —— Tipping Drill

5:45 - 5:50 P.M. —— Full-court defense-offense drill

5:50 ..................... —— Shoot free throws

Chart I

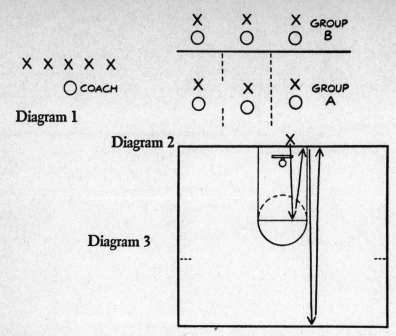

Diagram 1

Diagram 2

Diagram 3

switches off and is guarded in turn. No ball is used in this drill.

### Defensive Killer Drill

In this drill, all the players line up at the end of the floor and face one side. Using the defensive slide and facing the same side of the floor at all times, they slide to the free-throw line—back to the base line—out to the center-court line—and finally back to the base line again (See Diagram 3).

### Reaction Drill

We use several reaction drills in this part of the station. Knee boxing and perhaps a hand reaction drill as used in football are both excellent for this purpose.

### STATION II

Shooting drills are emphasized in this segment of the Crash Program.

### Half-Court Shooting Drill on the Move

In this drill, a player takes the ball, dribbles to mid-court and back toward the basket, shoots a jumper on the move, and then takes the rebound. He repeats this for five shots and then his partner does the same. Five or six may participate at any one time.

### Garbage Drill

Players are placed in groups of three: one tossing the ball, one shooting, and one resting. After three shots, each player changes positions. As illustrated in Diagram 4, four groups are placed around the basket, each member with his back to it. A puts the ball on the floor, rolling it to a position just short of B, who retrieves it and shoots. C is the resting player. When in one of the groups out in front, A and B fast-basket.

Although no one player may take any more than three shots, all four groups may go at the same time.

### STATION III

At this station, each player is drilled on passing and dribbling.

### Four-Corner Passing Drill

Two men (each with a ball) place themselves in the middle of the half-court, while one player positions himself in each corner. Each center player passes to the corner man, who returns the ball and moves in towards the middle. The center player then hands off the ball to him and takes up a position in the vacated corner. The new center player passes to the next corner, and the whole routine is repeated (Diagram 5).

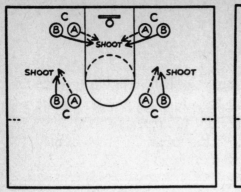 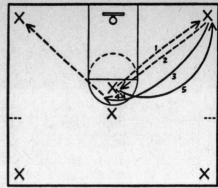

Diagram 4                    Diagram 5

Four balls may be used as the efficiency of the players increases.

### Dribble Obstacle Course

Cones are set up as in Diagram 6 for the players to dribble through. Each player is expected to weave around the single cones and pivot around the double ones.

### STATION IV

Here the players are trained in improving their rebounding skills.

### 1-on-1 Semi-Circle Drill

As illustrated in Diagram 7, a group of players (the shooters) form a semi-circle at a radius of about 21 feet from the basket. Two more players (the rebounders) are placed in the center on the free-throw line. A ball is shot at the basket, and the rebounder taking the ball becomes the offensive player. He passes the ball to a player in the semi-circle (who will shoot it), runs to the free-throw line, and waits for the rebound. The second rebounder—the one who did not get the ball—becomes the defensive player and tries to block the first rebounder until the ball gets out to the semi-circle. Then

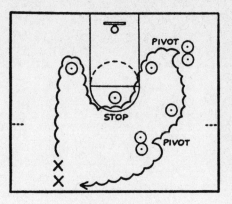 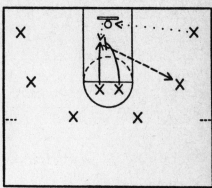

Diagram 6                    Diagram 7

he joins the first rebounder at the free-throw line, and they start again.

The rebounder who gets the ball initially must return to the free-throw line after passing the ball out to the shooters.

### Reaction Drill

Players are placed in two lines, each facing a partner in the line opposite. The coach positions himself in back of one line. At his signal, each player in the line *facing* him starts to move as though he were going in for the rebound, while the man between him and the coach tries to block him out.

### CONCLUSION

Of course, many other drills may be used in the Crash Program. Each drill we use is designed to contribute to all phases of basketball, as well as develop conditioning, reflexes, agility, and speed. We have had success with this program, feeling that as we refine it, we will gain additional benefits.